Take *Heart* & Teach

How to teach with excellence,
balance, and the joy of the Lord
(even when things are crazy)

Linda Kardamis

Published by:
Teach 4 the Heart, LLC
www.teach4theheart.com

ISBN: **978-0692092538**

Other books by Linda Kardamis
Create Your Dream Classroom
Teach Uplifted Devotions for Teachers

Table of Contents

A Note from the Author vii

Download Your Bonus Resources. x

Part 1: Take Heart in Classroom Management 1

Lesson 1: Chaos and Confusion. 2

Lesson 2: Kind or Strict? 7

Lesson 3: Shake It Up 10

Lesson 4: Follow the Leader. 14

Lesson 5: Sweat the Small Stuff 16

Lesson 6: Mental Wars. 18

Lesson 7: The Magic Words. 21

Lesson 8: Rapport - Schmapoor. 23

Lesson 9: From Toilet Poems to Christmas Cards. 25

Lesson 10: Down to the Root 28

Lesson 11: Enjoy the Journey 31

Lesson 12: A Drawer Full of Pantyhose 35

Lesson 13: Whole Brain Genius. 39

Lesson 14: Your Secret Weapon 42

Resources 44

Part 2: Take Heart and Find Balance.................45

Lesson 15: Liar, Liar 46

Lesson 16: You Need a Budget.......................50

Lesson 17: Do Not Disturb.........................54

Lesson 18: I Can't Think 57

Lesson 19: I Heart Procrastination...................61

Lesson 20: A Bag Full of Bricks 66

Lesson 21: Where the Rubber Meets the Road...........70

Lesson 22: But Wait, There's More! 75

Lesson 23: Praying for Balance 80

Resources 82

Part 3: Take Heart and Teach with Joy 83

Lesson 24: An Audience of One.......................84

Lesson 25: Gotta' Be God 86

Lesson 26: New Thoughts, New Joy...................90

Lesson 27: A Moment to Breathe.....................94

Lesson 28: Stress Busters 99

Lesson 29: The Principal's Office 104

Lesson 30: Attack of the Sauls 107

Lesson 31: The Complaint Department is Closed 114

Lesson 32: Growth Takes Time 121

Lesson 33: Prayer Changes YOU 124

Resources 126

Part 4: Take Heart and Make a Bigger Difference........**127**

Lesson 34: Why We Teach............................128

Lesson 35: Love Conquers All.........................130

Lesson 36: Apples Come from Apple Trees 133

Lesson 37: Facts and Opinions 136

Lesson 38: Creation, the Fall, and Redemption 141

Lesson 39: Walking with God 144

Lesson 40: Fake it Till You Make It? 148

Lesson 41: Teach for the Heart 151

Lesson 42: Making Disciples.........................154

Lesson 43: Freedom, Religion, and the 1ˢᵗ Amendment 160

Lesson 44: Praying Always...........................166

Resources 169

Conclusion 170

Appendix A: Consequence Ideas 171

Appendix B: Call-and-Response Sayings 175

Appendix C: Checklist Grading Form Example...........176

To Tim.
Thank you for loving me, supporting me, and following God's
leading, And thanks for hanging with the kids so I could write.
Without you, this book would not exist.

Acknowledgements

I praise and thank God for all He has done, all He has taught me, and how He has guided both Teach 4 the Heart and this book.

Thank you to Tim, my husband and partner, not only for carving out time for me to write but also for designing and laying out the book.

To my editor, Tyler Agnew, thank you for all the work you put into making this book read more smoothly.

And finally, to all of you who read and support Teach 4 the Heart, thank you from the bottom of my heart. You are not only the reason we wrote this book; you are also how we were *able* to write this book.

Thank you!

A Note from the Author

And let us not grow weary while doing good, for in due season we shall reap if we do not lose heart. —Galatians 6:9

As teachers, we can be weighed down by a myriad of challenges. Seemingly impossible students, ever-expanding stacks of grading, unrealistic expectations, and the exhaustion of the daily grind all conspire to make us lose heart. Sometimes we might even wonder why we wanted to teach in the first place.

Take heart, dear teacher, for God isn't done yet.

He's not done with your students, and He's not done with you. He sees each challenge, each frustration, each struggle, and He's using them to strengthen, equip, and grow us.

But growth takes time.

So don't be discouraged by the struggle or overwhelmed by the obstacles. Instead, trust in Him, depend on Him and wait on Him as He gradually makes us not only exemplary teachers but also channels through which He can work. Then we can say with the Psalmist:

I would have lost heart, unless I had believed that I would see the goodness of the Lord in the land of the living. Wait on the Lord; be of good courage, and He shall strengthen your heart. Wait, I say, on the Lord! –Psalm 27:13-14

My prayer is that this book will be a tool in His hands to help you grow as a teacher and learn to depend on Him more. In it, we'll tackle four aspects of teaching, discovering how to take heart and teach strong in His strength.

We'll begin with classroom management, the foundation on which a strong classroom is built. Then we'll tackle how to teach with balance—learning to wisely invest our time and energy so that we not only teach with excellence but also flourish in our other God-given roles. From there, we'll explore how to teach with His peace and joy, even when things are going wrong.

Armed with a strong classroom management plan, balanced by wise time-management, and centered through deep trust in and joy from Christ, you'll be equipped to make a bigger difference than ever. Thus, our final section will focus on how to maximize your impact and shine His light in your classroom.

As you read, remember that merely reading something will only get you so far. Instead, go the extra mile: peruse the pages and intentionally engage with this book. Get more out of the lessons by completing the accompanying journal prompts and then discussing them with fellow teachers—either in your own small group or in one of our online book clubs (**www.teach4theheart.com/bookclub**).

We've also included some bonus materials to help you implement what you're learning. You can grab them at **www.teach4theheart.com/takeheartbonus**.

Ready to dive in?

Let's get started.

Have I not commanded you? Be strong and of good courage; do not be afraid, nor be dismayed, for the LORD your God is with you wherever you go. —Joshua 1:9

Download Your Bonus Resources

We've prepared bonus resources for you to help you implement some of the strategies we discuss in the book. They're yours absolutely free at **www.teach4theheart.com/takeheartbonus**.

Part 1:
Take Heart in
Classroom Management

Let all things be done decently and in order. —I Corinthians 14:40

Strong classroom management is essential to effective teaching. Without it, little learning can take place.

If you're struggling to keep order, take heart. This section will help you create a conducive learning environment—a place where you can teach and your students can learn.

Lesson 1:
Chaos and Confusion

The bell rings. Chaos ensues. Chatter fills the room. A few students wander around. You have to admit: no one is paying attention to you. You raise your voice and no one can hear. You flick the lights. Still the noise continues. You wait. You flash the evil eye. You pray they will somehow stop talking. Finally, right as the class is mercifully starting to settle down, two tardy students flail into the room. Just like that, everything is out of control again.

If this sounds anything like a typical day for you, you are not alone. I've had my fair share of these moments. During my rookie year of teaching, I let too many things slide, and I was having major issues in my classroom by October. I remember trying to teach over the roar of students' private conversations and knowing this wasn't how teaching was supposed to look. To make matters worse, something pretty rough must've happened behind my back because I found myself having a lovely chat with the principal about how I needed to start controlling my classes.

"You need to muster some authority," he said.

Realizing my classroom was not what I wanted was discouraging and frustrating. But the wake-up call was timely. It marked the start of my classroom turnaround. I would love to tell you that by the next week my classes were orderly and on task. That's not the case. It took time for me to figure out an effective system, to gain confidence as a classroom manager, and to show the kids I was going to follow through and hold them accountable. But things did improve, and when I started the next year off right, my classroom was night-and-day better.

Don't give up if you're struggling to keep control of your class. Regaining control won't be easy, but it will be worth it when you have a controlled, effective classroom—one where your students are learning and where you actually enjoying teaching them.

We'll start with an overview of how to regain control and then dive deeper into specific strategies and techniques:

1. **Pray and rely on God.** God is there to help. He will guide you as you seek to develop an effective classroom. Pray constantly, and rely on Him for strength and wisdom.

2. **Take responsibility for your classroom**. The first step toward regaining control is to realize controlling your classroom is your responsibility. If you're blaming the students or the circumstances or anything else, you're giving yourself excuses not to change. You *can* control your classroom with the right techniques and attitude. Start by believing in yourself and accepting responsibility for your classroom.

3. **Create a strategy.** If you're going to control your classroom, you must develop a plan. As much as is humanly possible: plan, plan, plan. Write down what you will say when a student walks into class late. Predetermine what discipline you will administer when a student says something disrespectful. Jot down a course of action for when students are talking when you're teaching.

If you don't have a plan, you won't know what to do. The kids will see that and continue to take advantage of you.

Almost any plan is better than no plan, so don't get stuck waiting for the perfect solution. Try something. See how it goes. Better yet, ask advice from a veteran teacher at your school or in our Facebook discussion group. (You can request to join at **www.teach4theheart.com/group**.)

4. **Determine your consequences.** Positive reinforcement is essential. But if your classroom is out of control, positive motivation alone will not solve your problems. You simply must create consequences. Determine repercussions for the times a student fails to meet one of your expectations.

    Don't plan a harsh response for a student's first infraction. Doing so might make you hesitant to address issues (and isn't fair to your students either). Consider a formal warning system. For example, you could give a student a warning for the first infraction in the form of a name on the board or a post-it note on the desk. Then decide what reasonable consequence you will give for subsequent infractions. (See Appendix A for a list of consequence ideas.)

5. **Build your confidence.** Students can sense when you're not confident in your ability to discipline them. You might as well be wearing a sign that says, "Feel free to misbehave. I don't know what to do!" The first step in building your confidence is to finish writing out your plan. Then, practice your responses in front of a mirror until you're confident you can deliver them effectively.

6. **Plan a classroom shake-up.** Making changes in the middle of the school year is tough because your students are settled in their bad habits. Force a reset by conducting a classroom shake-up. We'll talk more about this in a future lesson, but the idea is to use actions, not words, to show students things will be different going forward.

7. **Address the first problem.** Your classroom shake-up will get your students' attention; it will not change anything unless you address the first problem. Whether the problem occurs two seconds after the bell or halfway into class, address the problem right away with your predetermined response. Keep in mind you don't have to hand out a punishment for every minor infraction. Simply address it. A quick "Olivia, remember to sharpen your pencil before class starts," shows you're paying attention and expect students to follow class procedures.

8. **Remain consistent.** Don't let your mood or your energy level affect how you deal with classroom issues. Stay steady. Teach students what to expect. Follow through with consequences. After a few weeks or months, you may be able to loosen up, but don't let anything go until you're confident the class is under control.

9. **Organize and develop efficiency.** If you're going to have an orderly classroom, you must systematize. You cannot waste class time. A two-minute lull in the middle of class is an open invitation for students to start wreaking havoc. Keep them busy. Don't afford them time for mischief. And be interesting! Most discipline problems happen when kids are bored.

10. **Show students you care.** Our kids must know we care about them. Invest in them, talk to them, empathize with their struggles, and show interest in the things they love. Spend extra time with your most challenging students. Intentionally engage them in conversations about non-school related topics whenever possible.

Journal/Discussion: What has been your biggest classroom management struggle? What have you learned that has helped you the most?

Lesson 2:
Kind or Strict?

"You're being too nice. You've got to toughen up."

Hearing these words from your administrator can be frustrating—and a bit confusing, too. Your students aren't listening to you. You're having trouble keeping order in your classroom. But must you stop being nice?

Or maybe you're on the other end of the spectrum. You're laying down the law. You'll ensure students respect you. You'd never be accused of being to too nice—you embody strictness.

Neither of these extremes are qualities of an effective teacher. To gain your students' respect and their buy-in, you must be both nice *and* strict. Balance is key. You must achieve an even demeanor. Keep kindness and extend empathy, all the while holding your students to high standards.

Keys to Maintaining the Right Demeanor:

1. **Teach with kindness and firmness.** The best teachers are personable, understanding, and even fun to be around. This doesn't mean they're pushovers. They handle issues with grace

and strength. Their students know they mean business. They also know their teacher keeps their best interest at heart.

2. **Maintain high expectations.** Don't think you're helping students when you lower expectations. Instead, believe in your students. Trust their abilities. Call out the best in them. Expect greatness and hold them to lofty standards.

3. **Focus on being respected instead of being liked.** If you're worried about whether or not your students like you, you'll end up making poor decisions and soon lose your students' respect. Instead, earn their trust. Excel as a teacher. Learn to manage your classroom well. Construct high standards, and hold them accountable. They'll probably look back at you and say, "Wow, s/he was a great teacher!"

4. **Show up for students each day.** Think back to your all-time favorite teachers. You knew they cared about you, didn't you? They paid attention when you talked. The best teachers are present. They don't constantly look at their phone or the clock throughout the day but instead model standards of respect. Be that teacher for your students.

5. **View yourself as your students' mentor, not their friend.** You should care about students and want to be involved in their lives. But you must take the role of adviser, not friend. A mentor guides students without acting like a peer.

6. **Be friendly. Don't be familiar.** Be friendly and open in your interactions with students, but avoid being familiar. For example, if a student shares with you that they got to go snorkeling on their recent vacation, a friendly response may sound like this: "Wow, Adam, it sounds like you and your

family had a great time! I love snorkeling. Did you get to see any turtles?" On the other hand, a familiar response would be, "Dude, that's sweet! I'm so jealous!" See the difference?

Journal/Discussion: Do you lean toward being nice or strict? What can you tweak to find a better balance?

Lesson 3:
Shake It Up

Do you have a problem area in your classroom? You know, that one activity where everything seems to fall apart? Maybe you have trouble settling your class down when they return from lunch, or maybe things get a little crazy when you ask them to exchange papers.

We often find ourselves trying to survive these hectic moments. But what if there were a way to fix these problem areas? One thing's for sure: if we keep doing what we're doing, nothing will change. So maybe it's time you shook things up.

A classroom shake-up uses actions instead of words to show students the class is heading in a new direction. The goal is to get your students' attention. Make them think, *what's going on?* Forcing a reset allows you to make changes mid-year. Before we get into the details, let me give you an example:

I was talking to a teacher who was having trouble with kids misbehaving as they put away their coats and bookbags in the morning. None of her interventions helped, so I suggested a shake-up. Her students would typically hang their coats and bookbags on a moving cart stationed outside their classroom. The problem was that they goofed off and caused all kinds of trouble in the process. It was part of the routine.

I suggested she hide the cart the next day.

The students were dumbfounded.

"Where's the cart?" one asked.

Their heads swiveled, looking down the hall.

"Someone stole it!" another said.

They asked a lot of questions, and even caused a bit of a ruckus. But here's the kicker: she had their attention. After nonchalantly ignoring their inquiries for a few minutes, she then explained the situation.

"The coat rack is gone because we were having way too many problems with it," she said. "Now, we're going to try something new. From now on, instead of going straight to the coat rack, you will immediately bring all of your belongings into the classroom. You will sit at your desks until I call for you to go hang up your coats two at a time."

She went on, explaining her expectations in vivid, step-by-step detail. Afterward, she was *extremely* vigilant as the students attempted the new process for the first time. She corrected any small misbehavior. She addressed anything not done exactly as expected. She was kind but firm, too. She continued her vigilance for a few days as her students perfected the new procedure.

See how it works?

Now, I realize moving a piece of classroom furniture isn't the answer to every problem. But there is a creative solution for the issues in your class.

How to Create a Classroom Shake-Up

1. **Identify your problem area.** Ask yourself what situation, circumstance, or routine causes the most problems in your classroom. Or, you might need to consider a general shake-up to reset your whole classroom.

2. **Determine a better procedure for problem areas.** Imagine how you want routines to work from now on. Think particularly about what was causing the problems and what you can do differently to avoid them.

3. **Find a way to shake it up.** Contemplate what you can do to show your students you are making a clean break from the old procedure and implanting a new one. Consider taking something out of the room or skipping a part of your routine. Or, simply lock your classroom door and don't let your students in.

4. **Make your move.** Watch calmly during the chaos of your classroom shake-up. Don't explain why until your students notice. Don't respond until they ask questions.

5. **Explain and teach the procedure.** This is not the time to lecture your students. Instead, kindly but firmly explain the new procedure. Then practice it with them.

6. **Vigilantly correct every misbehavior or mistake.** If you miss this step, chaos will return in no time. After your shake-up, don't let anything go. Look for that first misbehavior and correct it right away. Continue to correct and instruct until the task is flawlessly completed.

7. **Have students redo the procedure.** If the students didn't

follow the new routine correctly, have them try again. It might feel like you're wasting time, but you'll actually be saving a ton of time in the future by showing them you're serious. Redoing the task will also help them remember the right way to do it.

Journal/Discussion: What is your problem area? What can you do to shake it up?

Lesson 4:
Follow the Leader

Procedures are paramount. They help your class run efficiently, they give students a sense of confidence and security, and they help prevent discipline issues. But whether it's the first week of school or the middle of the year, how you teach students procedures will have a huge impact on how successful they are.

When you implement a new procedure, it is not enough to tell students what you expect of them. You have to practice—and practice everything.

The 4-Step Process for Teaching Procedures

1. **Give clear, specific directions.** The first time you tell your students to pass in papers, you cannot just say, "Please pass in your papers." If you do, you may get a stack of papers, but it will come with a side of chaos. So specify your directions. Say something like this instead:

   "We are going to pass our papers in. Those at the back of the row will pass theirs forward first. Please wait to pass in your paper until you have the stack. When it gets to the front, Makenzie will pass them to Jared who will pass them to Steve who will give the whole pile to Alex. Alex, please paper clip the stack and place them on my desk."

2. **Have students run through the procedure.** After you give the directions, have the students complete the task. As they do, check if they are doing everything correctly.

3. **Patiently correct.** The chance that students will pass in the papers correctly the first time, despite your perfectly planned explanation, is about two percent. Your students will get it mostly right, but Jon won't wait for the person behind him, Elana will put hers upside down, and Alex will forget what to do with the stack when it arrives. When you see mistakes, gently remind students how to properly complete the task.

4. **Try again and again.** Yes, that's right. Redo it. It may feel like nit-picking, but this is where the magic happens. When you ask students to reattempt the procedure, you not only show them you mean what you say, but you also cement the new procedure in their minds.

As you practice your procedures, here's a few tips to keep in mind:

• Be kind when you correct the students. and don't make them feel foolish. Say things like, "I know it's a lot to remember, but..." or "Thank you for...Don't forget to...."

• Plan to cover less material the first week of school so you have time to teach and practice procedures. Again, you're not wasting time. The minutes you invest in teaching procedures will save you hours throughout the year.

Journal/Discussion: Why is practicing procedures important?

Lesson 5:
Sweat the Small Stuff

It's easy to ignore small misbehavior: a child who "doesn't hear" you calling or students whispering during a lesson. We think it's no big deal, and we move on with our day. We have more pressing concerns. And we're not supposed to sweat the small stuff, right?

During my first year of teaching, I let a lot of little things go because I didn't think they were worth worrying about, and I didn't want to hand out punishments for tiny infractions. But once students saw I wasn't going to correct them for whispering, they started talking whenever they wanted. When I didn't correct one student for blurting out an answer, soon everyone was shouting out responses. Pandemonium quickly broke out. My issues grew. By the time I realized my mistake, reining in my out-of-control class was an immense challenge.

So are we supposed to sweat the small stuff? I would say yes— at least until you don't need to anymore. When you have your students' respect and your classroom is a well-oiled machine, you can afford students some leeway. But when you're trying to reset the tone for your classroom, you must address the small stuff, or you'll find yourself right back where you were. Here's why:

1. **Little problems don't stay little.** It's a sad fact, but it's true—if we allow small issues to go uncorrected, they will expand into bigger problems.

2. **If you don't deal with them now, you'll have to deal with them later.** We often feel we don't have time to deal with a minor issue right now. We can't kid ourselves. If we don't deal with the small problem now, we're going to have to deal with larger problems later on.

3. **It takes longer to retrain than to train.** Nipping a problem in the bud may take time and energy, but not nearly as much as it will to retrain your students after you've allowed them to develop bad habits.

4. **You can deal with small problems kindly.** One reason I let so much go was that I thought my only option was to hand out punishments. That's not the case. Sometimes a simple redirection or an explanation of what behavior is proper is all that's needed. The student just needs to see that the behavior is not acceptable and will not be permitted.

5. **Kids thrive on consistency.** The more consistent we are, the better. Kids understand and appreciate consistency because they know exactly what is expected of them. If today a little backtalk is ignored but tomorrow they get slapped with a detention, they will be confused and frustrated, and our efforts to instill good habits and character will be hindered. The more consistent we are on the front end, the more quickly our students will learn the lessons we want to teach them.

Journal/Discussion: Have you made the mistake of letting the little things go? What happened when you did?

Lesson 6:
Mental Wars

Correcting students is hard for me. When I first started teaching I had to give myself a mental pep-talk before I could even give a small "Oliver, please don't tip back in your chair" correction. And I may or may not have had to call my husband to help me get up the nerve to hand out my first detention.

Even as I got more used to correcting students, I still struggled with consistency. I would stand at the board knowing I needed to address a problem. All the while, a fight raged inside my head:

I need to say something to that student.

But I don't want to.

This is important. Just do it.

But I don't want to.

You know you need to. There's nothing to be afraid of. Just do it.

But....I really don't want to.

There's something inside of us that doesn't want to deal with problems we know we should handle. But even though consistency is hard, we must make it a priority.

Here are some steps that can help us be more consistent in our discipline:

1. **Get clear on why consistency is essential.** If we don't deal with the problems, they're not going to go away. Instead, they'll worsen. Spend time imagining how out-of-control your classroom will be if you let things go. Consider how much harder it's going to be to deal with these behaviors if you let them become bad habits.

2. **Decide ahead of time.** Instead of going through an internal debate when an issue arises, determine beforehand that you will simply act. Yes, this is easier said than done. But your resolve will make it easier to follow through in the moment.

3. **When the problem arises, don't debate. Just act.** You know it's important, and you've determined your plan ahead of time. Now, just do it. Don't allow an internal debate to start. When you see a problem, act right away.

4. **If you mess up, catch the next problem.** If you do fail to correct a problem (and chances are this will happen), don't get discouraged, and don't believe the lie that you've ruined everything. Instead, determine that you are *absolutely* going to deal with the next issue—no letting it slide. By doing so, you make your mistake a small bump in the road instead of letting it snowball into a huge mess.

5. **Pray, pray, pray.** We often pray for help and wisdom as teachers, but why not specifically ask for help in being consistent? We can't do it without Him.

6. **Get an accountability partner.** Find a fellow teacher or family member that will check in with you periodically and ask how you're doing with consistency.

Journal/Discussion: Why do you think it's so hard to be consistent? Why does consistency matter?

Lesson 7:
The Magic Words

We've all seen it happen. We try to correct a student—or give them basic instruction—and they jump to the conclusion that we're "yelling" at them or that they're in trouble. Soon what should've been a ten-second correction has escalated into a ridiculous, drawn-out argument, topped off when concerned parents show up the next day — having been told you "don't like Johnny and are picking on him."

Enter four magic words containing the power to dissolve tension and eliminate at least half of the arguments in your classroom.

And those words are: "**You're not in trouble.**"

I used this phrase all the time when I was teaching, but was reminded of their power the other day when working with 6th graders at church. This class has that one student whose goal is to cause as many disruptions as humanly possible. And, of course, he must correct you as the teacher when you ask him to be quiet but not the person behind him. You know the type.

Class started. Then stalled at his disruption.

"Please stop," I asked, to which he sent back a loud, defensive response—building another layer of distraction. The lesson continued. The disruptions persisted. The cycle continued. Then, I remembered the magic words: "Andrew, you're not in trouble, but you're causing distractions. Please sit in the back. Thanks."

The incredible result? No "why are you picking on me?" No "but Alex is talking too!" No, "but that's not fair!" I might've had to put on my "I'm serious" face, but he got up and moved to the back without causing any more incidents.

Point for the magic words.

So the next time Camden gets defensive when you ask him to stop talking and focus, say something like, "Camden, you're not in trouble. You just need to get back to work. Thanks." And see what happens.

"You're not in trouble," won't work one hundred percent of the time, but it will make a huge difference. Just be sure to couple it with a calm tone and pleasant disposition and wait for the magic to happen.

Journal/Discussion: Have you ever used the phrase, "You're not in trouble" in your classroom? What else have you found helps ease your students' tension?

Lesson 8:
Rapport - Schmapoor

I know teachers who champion the importance of developing rapport with students. They claim rapport can be the difference between an out-of-control class and a respectful one. They say once you develop a bond with a student, that you'll be amazed how dedicated and loyal they become.

Just for kicks, let's say I don't believe them. Let's assume I think rapport is overrated, and more, I believe it might just be something you need to avoid at all cost. To that end, I'm sharing seven easy ways to destroy any rapport you might have inadvertently built up with your students.

7 Easy Ways to Destroy Rapport

1. **Make sure you're always right.** If you want to frustrate your students, insist you're right, even when you're wrong. Never apologize when you make a mistake or lose your temper.

2. **Cut off all avenues of appeal.** Don't let your students appeal any of your decisions. You are the teacher — the authority. Do not let them question you. Ever.

3. **Never laugh (especially at yourself).** If you want to be taken seriously, never smile. Never use humor. And, above all, never laugh at yourself.

4. **Turn in students for discipline without talking to them.** To be a top-notch rapport-killer, go behind your students back and turn in their names for detentions without saying anything to them. The look on their unsuspecting faces when they receive the slip from the office will be priceless!

5. **Yell at your students.** Next time your students are misbehaving, scream at them. Go off on a rant. It's a sure bet to kill your rapport in a heartbeat, especially if you remember rule #1.

6. **Accuse a student when you kinda-sorta-probably know what happened.** Next time you think Clara *may* have cheated, don't wait until you're sure. Accuse her right away. Make sure you're insistent she *did* do it and isn't going to get away with it!

7. **Put on a façade.** While this might not make a big difference right away, stick with it and it will definitely pay off. It's the most powerful way to destroy your rapport. Simply pretend to be something you're not, or hold your students to different standards than you have for yourself. Rapport-destroying gold!

Journal/Discussion: While we had a little fun addressing this topic in a tongue-and-cheek way, the sad truth is that we can too easily destroy our rapport. Did you recognize yourself in any of these seven rapport destroyers? What do you want to do differently?

Lesson 9:
From Toilet Poems to
Christmas Cards

Can you picture him or her—that kid who's always driving you crazy? The incessant talking, the attitude, the disrespect.

Why can't they be absent every day?

Each year, we seem to be blessed with a kid or two who tests our patience. Yes, I said *blessed*, and I actually don't mean it sarcastically. The student who begins as our biggest frustration often turns into our greatest blessing.

I remember one student whose goal must have been to frustrate me as much as possible. She would run full force into me every chance she got. (Was she trying to knock me down?) We discussed such topics as why writing a poem about a toilet was inappropriate (you can't make this stuff up), and she would walk away mid-sentence. I honestly thought she was a lost cause.

But the next year things gradually started to change. I noticed less and less attitude. Soon I realized we hadn't had a problem in weeks. Before long she was smiling, respectful, and came by my room just to talk. By our third year together, she matured enough to tell me, "I can't believe I acted that way. What was I thinking?"

She became a delight to teach, and her thoughtful Christmas cards and graduation announcement graced my fridge years after she left my classroom.

Not every story ends this way, but God has called us to impact each student as much as we can. So don't be discouraged, and don't give up hope. Our God can do incredible things. When a student is driving you crazy, don't build walls. Try these ideas instead:

1. **Love them.** Loving our students isn't always easy, but love is a choice. True love is given when it's not deserved. God loves us even though we are undeserving, and we must do the same for our students.

2. **Pray for them.** Obviously, we are praying that God will work to change their heart, but God also uses our prayers to change us—to give us a love that we didn't think we could have.

3. **Pour into students.** Show them you care. In *The 7 Habits of Highly Effective People,* Stephen Covey gives the metaphor of an emotional bank account. If we are making lots of "withdrawals" in the form of correction and discipline, we must "deposit" even more by encouraging them, noticing their successes, and showing them we care.

4. **Find out more about them.** Talk to their former teachers and their parents to discover what makes them tick. Is there a particular challenge they are facing? What do they enjoy? What helps them succeed?

5. **Talk to students.** Have conversations as often as possible. Yes, talk to them about their attitude and behavior but also find time to ask about their interests outside of school. Many teachers witness incredible turnarounds using the 2 x 10

method: simply chatting with your most challenging student for **two** minutes a day for **ten** days.

6. **Speak to their heart.** Don't look only at their outward behavior. Reach for the root of the problems by speaking to their hearts.

7. **Seek advice.** If you're at your wit's end, seek advice from a fellow teacher or administrator. Our Christian Teachers' Discussion Group is designed to help with challenges like these. (Go to **www.teach4theheart.com/group** to join.)

8. **Be consistent.** Don't lower your standards or let them get away with misbehavior. Be consistent in your expectations and your follow through, but show them you care every step of the way.

9. **Be patient.** Sometimes we forget that growth takes time. We want to see results right away, but the fruits of our labor might not show up for months or even years. Don't give up on your students, and don't get discouraged when the changes don't happen as quickly as you'd like. Be patient. You never know whose name might show up in five years on a Christmas card.

Journal/Discussion: What do you want to do differently this week with your most challenging students?

Lesson 10:
Down to the Root

When it comes to dealing with discipline problems, we have a few choices.

1. We can ignore it.

2. We can yell at the student.

3. We can give an eloquent lecture.

4. We can calmly tell the student to correct their behavior.

5. We can assign a consequence and move on.

While some of these options are plainly better than others, none of them help much when you're facing an ongoing issue. That's because these are all surface solutions—they don't get to the root of the problem.

If we desire lasting change, we must take the time to find out what's truly causing the issue. Is Camden cheating because he's afraid of failure? Is Priscilla the class clown because she thinks that's how she'll make friends? Does Elias not do his homework because he's too busy playing video games?

When we figure out the root issue, we can attack the problem at its core. And when we can help the student overcome the underlying problem, we'll start to see real progress and real improvement. The biggest challenge, though, is figuring out what problem lies underneath. It's not always obvious, and it sometimes takes a bit of work to discover the underlying issue.

How to Find the Root Cause of Discipline Problems

1. **Take time to talk to the student.** Yes, you are busy, but the time you invest in figuring out the root issue will pay off when you start seeing improvement in your student's behavior. Take time to talk to them—and not only about the problems they're having. Get to know them, show them you care, and start to develop rapport with them.

2. **Ask questions and wait for answers.** When you talk to them about their behavior, ask questions and wait for their answers. If they're standing there staring at the floor, don't fill the space with a lecture. Instead, sit quietly and wait for a response. If needed, ask a follow-up question, but you must get them to join the conversation because you're never going to figure out the underlying issue if you're the one doing all the talking.

3. **Talk to the parents.** Share with the parents how you are trying to discover the underlying problem that's causing their child's inappropriate behavior, and ask them what they're observing at home. Listen carefully to their responses and keep them involved throughout the process.

4. **Seek first to understand.** During these conversations, seek first to understand, then to be understood. Actively listen and see the situation from the student's or parent's point of view *before* you try to explain your own point of view.

5. **Coordinate with other faculty or staff members who may have additional insight.** If you're stumped, coordinate with other teachers that have taught the student or any administrative personnel who may be working with him or her. They may have gained some insight that could be helpful to you.

Once you've found out the underlying cause(s), you can work together with the student and parents to address the true problem instead of just the surface issues.

Journal/Discussion: Why must we get to the root cause of ongoing discipline issues?

Lesson 11:
Enjoy the Journey

When faced with a roomful of rambunctious 7th-graders
and no way to command their attention, my mentor teacher
recommended a simple warning system: when students are
talking out or being disruptive, write their name on the board as
a warning. If they receive three warnings in the same class period,
assign a consequence.

This simple warning system was exactly what I needed to turn
my classroom around. It allowed me to address small behavior
issues without slamming students with detentions. The individual
responsibility this system evoked helped students self-correct and
stay on task.

I often recommend a similar system to teachers who are struggling
with classroom management—suggesting they tweak it by using
Class Dojo or sticky notes if they're not comfortable putting
names on the board. As I've shared this technique, I've found the
opinions on warning systems and behavior charts are vast and
varied. Some teachers, like me, see their value. But others share
how glad they are that they finally ditched them and make it
sound like you need to ditch yours, too. So who's right?

If you're caught up in the confusion (and the guilt) of the behavior chart wars, I hope to offer a unique perspective most people are missing. Hopefully, you'll feel freed to do what is best for your students and your classroom.

First, a few thoughts about warning systems and behavior charts:

• **They can help keep your class under control.** If you're having trouble keeping your class in order, warning systems and behavior charts are a great tool to utilize. They provide students with the visual reminder that they need to correct their behavior, and you have a plan in place—giving you confidence that you know how to work your plan.

• **They are not the end-all-be-all.** Any teacher will tell you behavior charts do not solve all classroom problems. That's because all they can do is track behavior, not help kids confront the root issues. They're a tool, but they're not a perfect solution.

• **They have their downsides.** I don't buy into the whole "Johnny's self-esteem is hurt by having to move his pin to red" thing. (I find that what the Bible says about self-esteem is about 180 degrees different than what society says). However, these charts *can* cause severe stress for kids—or make them feel frustrated or defeated when they're genuinely trying but still messing up.

So maybe behavior charts aren't the best solution after all. They don't help us build relationships or reach our students' hearts. Should we ditch them altogether?

My answer: it depends.

Before you stone me for being cryptic, let's look at two vital truths:

Truth #1: You can't build strong relationships with your students if your class is out of control.

The most effective teachers have strong relationships with their students. If your class is out of control, you'll struggle to build those relationships. You'll also have a class full of students who aren't learning, and you're going to feel like pulling your hair out every day.

New teachers especially tend to get themselves in trouble by trying to get their students to like them before they establish any authority. It sounds good in theory, but it doesn't work well in reality. To have strong relationships with your students, you must first be able to control and manage your class.

Truth #2: Teaching is a journey.

The teacher you are right now is not the same teacher you will be in five years. That's okay.

To one day have a classroom that runs efficiently without a behavior chart is an admirable goal, but most first-year teachers are going to have a hard time managing their classroom without a structured behavior plan. There are too many nuances, and they don't have enough confidence.

For example, when I started teaching I was nervous about dealing with discipline problems. So I didn't deal with them. Before long my students were running the show. I was ineffective. How could I be anything else? A structured behavior plan—including the warning system—saved me. It was the right call.

A few years later, however, a formal system wasn't as necessary. I used it to set the right tone the first few weeks of school and then phased it out for most of my classes. Why the change? I had the experience and confidence to deal with whatever happened. My students saw I was on top of things and responded without needing a formal behavior system.

The point? **Whether or not you should use a behavior chart might depend on where you are in your teaching journey.**

If you're new to teaching, or if you've been struggling with classroom management, this tool might be what you need to start the year off right. Pair it with compassion, in-depth conversations, and a focus on building strong relationships, and you should be good to go. In a few years, you can re-evaluate and see if you still need it.

If you've been using a behavior chart for twenty years, maybe it's time to take a second look. Maybe the experience, confidence, and wisdom you've gained can be better put to use under a different system; or perhaps you should start the year with a behavior chart but phase it out after a month or two.

As you make your decision, keep in mind that it's better to be an effective, behavior-chart-using teacher than a my-class-is-out-of-control, non-behavior-chart-using teacher. But if you can be more effective without one, maybe it's time for a change.

Journal/Discussion: What do you think? Do you use a warning system or behavior chart? Will they help you keep control or are you ready to move beyond them?

Lesson 12:
A Drawer Full of Pantyhose

If you ask ten teachers whether or not dressing professionally is essential, you'll get a variety of answers. To some, the answer is an emphatic *yes*. But if you look at successful teachers who manage to wear jeans, you might think the answer is *not necessarily*.

Does it matter what we wear as teachers? Should we focus on comfort and ease-of-movement or should we put forth the effort to dress more professionally? The answer: *it depends.*

In certain situations, the right attire may be the difference between success and utter failure. But for others, the difference professional clothing makes is practically nonexistent and may cause more problems than it helps.

Every teacher should look nice and, of course, dress modestly. We should be good examples to our students, and we shouldn't be distracting with our wardrobe (unless it's spirit week, of course). But the question here is whether or not we need to bust out the suits and blazers every day. Do guys need a tie? Do ladies need a drawer full of pantyhose? Or are tasteful capris and a semi-casual top occasionally acceptable?

Once again: *it depends.*

We should view the need to dress professionally on a bit of a sliding scale. There are multiple factors that affect this, so you can't necessarily look at the other teachers in your school and do exactly what they do.

You should probably dress more professionally...

1. **The younger you are.** When I was fresh out of college, it didn't matter what the veteran teachers at my school wore. I was young—really young. I needed to look like a teacher, and dress was a meaningful distinction, proven every time we had a dress down day and parents thought I was a student.

2. **The less you've been teaching.** That first year, professional dress can be crucial—both in how you portray yourself to your students and in the confidence it gives you. Once you've been teaching for twenty years—well, it may not be as critical.

3. **The earlier it is in the school year.** Even if you're a seasoned veteran in your mid-fifties who has it all together, the first day of school brings new students who don't know you from Adam. Therefore, dressing professionally at the start of school is always a must. First impressions still matter.

4. **The older your students are.** If you're teaching preschool, your students will not pay much attention to your dress, and dressing professionally won't make much of a difference. On the other hand, if you teach high school (or even middle school), dress matters much more, especially if you're somewhat close to them in age.

5. **The more parents are involved.** When you meet with parents, you want them to see you as a competent professional. That means when it's time for parent-teacher conferences,

orientation, or open house, you should probably step up the level of your dress by a notch or two.

6. **The less you have a natural air of authority.** Some people exude authority, and students start shaking in their boots simply by looking at them. That is not me. I am petite, young, and naturally soft-spoken. I have to develop my authority through other means—and professional dress is one of them.

7. **The more formal your school is.** Finally, the culture of your school is a big factor. In some schools, acceptable dress for the men is nothing short of a suit and tie. At others, wearing a button-down shirt makes you seem uber-professional. Take this into account, but remember that it's not the only factor to consider.

And since we all know how helpful visuals are, we could picture it like this:

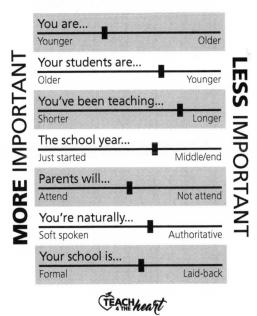

When Should Teachers Dress
PROFESSIONALLY?

MORE IMPORTANT — LESS IMPORTANT

You are...
Younger / Older

Your students are...
Older / Younger

You've been teaching...
Shorter / Longer

The school year...
Just started / Middle/end

Parents will...
Attend / Not attend

You're naturally...
Soft spoken / Authoritative

Your school is...
Formal / Laid-back

TEACH 4 THE *heart*

Journal/Discussion: Where do you fall on the spectrum? How essential is professional dress for your teaching situation? Would it help you to dress more professionally?

Lesson 13:
Whole Brain Genius

Sometimes there's a class that's—how can we say this nicely?—*challenging*. You've tried everything you can think of, and they still don't want to learn.

Enter whole brain teaching. This method, created by Chris Biffle, has helped thousands of teachers not only regain control but also get their students excited about learning. I don't agree with a hundred percent of his ideas (I'm more a fan of individual responsibility as opposed to class punishments and rewards), but there's no question he's on to something. Some of his ideas are pure genius.

To explain how whole brain teaching works would take way more time than we have today, but if a picture will save 1,000 words, a video will probably save 5,000. So pause a moment and head to **teach4theheart.com/wholebrain** to watch a quick video clip of Chris Biffle *showing* how whole brain teaching works.

What I Love About Whole Brain Teaching

1. **Students are actively engaged in learning.** Asking students to teach each other is genius. You don't have to do this all the time, but consider incorporating it occasionally. Not only are students engaged, but they also develop a deeper understanding, and you can discover and correct misconceptions.

2. **You can quiet the class in three seconds.** I spent years trying to figure out how to calm my class—flicking lights, holding up my hand, standing quietly, calling for attention—I tried it all. I wish I had known about the power of class-response sayings. The simple *class–yes* is genius because when the students say, "Yes," they automatically stop their own conversation to join in with the response. If you don't use anything else from whole brain teaching, you should try this. (By the way, there are more options than *class-yes*. See Appendix B for a list of call-and-response sayings.)

3. **The rules are genius.** If you're struggling to come up with class rules, borrow whole brain teaching's:

    • Follow directions quickly.

    • Raise your hand for permission to speak.

    • Raise your hand for permission to leave your seat.

    • Make smart choices.

    • Keep your dear teacher happy.

We don't have time to go into all of the advantages of these rules and how you can teach them to your students, but I link to a special series of articles Christ wrote at **teach4theheart.com/ wholebrain**. You can also grab his book *Whole Brain Teaching for Challenging Kids (and the rest of your class, too!)*

Journal/Discussion: Have you tried any whole-brain teaching elements in your classroom? What would you like to try?

Lesson 14:
Your Secret Weapon

I hope this section has given you strategies and ideas to improve your classroom management and create a more conducive learning environment—one where you can teach, and your students can learn. But if all we talk about is techniques and methods, we're not tapping into the greatest source of power and change:

Prayer.

How often do we view prayer as a last resort? *We've tried everything we can think of, so all we can do now is pray.*

But shouldn't we go to prayer first? Shouldn't we beseech God daily to transform our classrooms, to work in our students' heart and guide us to deal with each situation wisely?

If you remember nothing else from this book, remember this: you need God, and you need prayer.

He alone can move when we're at a loss, reaching into lives that seem hopeless, transforming them when we thought nothing could. He alone can guide us, filling us with His Spirit, equipping us to meet each challenge with patience, grace, and wisdom. He can do all this, and more. But have we asked Him?

Let's pray right now.

Journal/Put it into Practice: Pray right now for your classroom, your students, and yourself as their teacher. Here are some things you might pray for:

- That your students will be motivated, focused, and on-task

- That your students would feel safe and loved in your classroom

- That God would give you wisdom to properly handle various situations that arise in your classroom

- That God would give you the right words as you teach so that you will be effective, engaging, and relevant

- Finally, pray by name for your students, especially the ones who most frustrate you.

Resources

Check out these resources for more help with classroom management:

FREE Classroom Management MiniCourse: 3 Days to Regain Control

Need a little help putting it all together? This minicourse will give you more details and ideas on how to use a classroom shake-up to regain control of your classroom.

Join for free at **www.teach4theheart.com/minicourse.**

Classroom Management 101 Online Course

Classroom management is nuanced, and, unfortunately, one missing element can throw off your best efforts. Classroom Management 101 is a complete, organized system that ensures you don't miss any of the crucial aspects. We walk you step-by-step through the process of developing and implementing a strong classroom management plan.

Find out more at **www.teach4theheart.com/cm101.**

Part 2:
Take Heart and Find Balance

Look carefully then how you walk, not as unwise but as wise, making the best use of the time, because the days are evil. –Ephesians 5:15-16 (ESV)

Teaching is an incredible calling, but if you let it, it will take over your entire life and head you straight towards burnout.

If you are overwhelmed and exhausted, take heart. In this section, you'll learn to wisely invest your time and energy so that you not only teach with excellence but also flourish in the other roles God has given you.

Lesson 15:
Liar, Liar

Do you ever feel like teaching is taking over your life? You're overwhelmed. Stressed. You feel guilty for neglecting your family while at school then feel guilty for neglecting school while at home. You desperately need some balance in your life.

Chances are, you're believing a few lies—lies that get into your heads and prevent you from finding the balance you need. Let's reject these lies and replace them with truths that will free us to start making changes in our lives.

1. **Lie: Teachers are always working on school stuff at home. It's just how it is.**

   Truth: Lots of teachers have learned how to get everything done without letting it take over their lives. You can too.

   While you might need to take some work home, you shouldn't be working constantly, and school shouldn't be taking over your entire life. Many teachers have learned how to get their grading and lesson plans done in a reasonable amount of time, leaving time for their family and their personal growth. There are solutions.

2. **Lie: If I work fewer hours, I won't be as effective.**

   Truth: If you learn to be more efficient, you can be more effective in less time.

   Finding balance is not about letting our work go undone. It's about finding ways to be more efficient and intentional with the time you have so that you can get all your vital tasks done in a reasonable amount of time.

3. **Lie: I can jam-pack every minute of my day.**

   Truth: You desperately need margin in your life.

   If you're constantly running from the moment you get up to the moment your head hits the pillow, you're going to face some severe long-term consequences. Yes, there are jam-packed days here and there, and even crazy weeks from time to time. But this cannot be your normal, or your mood, health, and energy levels will suffer. You might even be headed straight for burnout. You need margin—space—in your life. Space to think, space to pray, space to enjoy teaching, life, and your family.

4. **Lie: The only way I'll find balance is if my school changes its crazy expectations.**

   Truth: You (and only you) can create balance in your life.

   Your school may have you teaching more classes, filling out more paperwork, or overseeing more extra-curricular activities than you'd prefer. Here's the truth though: it's up to you to create balance in your life, regardless of your situation. Even if your situation is less than ideal, you can move in the right direction. So don't let this lie be an excuse.

5. **Lie: There's nothing I can do. I can't work any faster.**

   Truth: Forget faster. You must be more intentional, focused and efficient.

   If you're trying to work faster, you're missing the point. It's not about magically becoming speedier. It's about learning to focus, to be intentional about where you spend your time, and to be efficient when you are working. We'll dive deeper into how to do this later in this section.

6. **Lie: Next year will be better.**

   Truth: Next year will present new challenges and will be better only if you make changes.

   If you're a first-year teacher, you can be fairly confident that next year will be better. Of course, the first year teaching new curriculum is always tough, too. But don't fall into the trap of assuming next year will be better and not making the changes needed to find balance. Your work may be easier in some ways next year, but there will most likely be new challenges and new responsibilities that will vie for your time. So don't simply hope next year will be better. Make changes to ensure it will be.

7. **Lie: I can do it all.**

   Truth: When you say *yes* to one thing, you say *no* to another.

   This is true in all aspects of life. When we say *yes* to one thing we are, by default, saying *no* to something else. What's tough is we may or may not realize what we're saying *no* to. A *yes* might steal time from focusing on your marriage or relaxing with your kids. A *yes* might even affect aspects of teaching, like having time to plan a cool lesson or talk with a student who needs advice. This doesn't mean we should start saying *no* to every opportunity. It does mean that we need to be intentional with our decisions and realize what we're saying *no* to when we agree to something else.

8. **Lie: Once I achieve balance, I'm golden.**

    Truth: Balance requires work and constant adjustment.

    Once we start pursuing balance, this lie can creep in and make us feel frustrated or even guilty that we haven't arrived yet. But the truth is that balance is not something we achieve and be done with. Instead, it's something we're always working on. It requires constant adjustments whenever one area of our life starts to get out of whack. So don't let that bother you. Embrace the imbalance that is inherently part of finding balance.

Journal/Discussion: Which lies have you believed? What truths do you need to replace them with?

Lesson 16:
You Need a Budget

When most people hear the word *budget*, they run for the hills, but I find some type of twisted pleasure in working with our family's budget. Maybe it's the math teacher in me, but forcing all the numbers into their proper place and seeing everything worked out and organized creates a little happy place for my soul.

Whether you think I'm crazy or love budgeting too, you can learn a lot about managing your time by taking some cues from good budgeting practices. Just as having a plan for your money is key to finding financial freedom, so planning your time is key to finding freedom and balance in your life. Using time wisely is what makes us truly rich — rich in relationships and rich in enjoyment of all God has given us.

5 Ways to Budget Your Time Wisely

1. **Spend your time on paper first.**

   Financial budgets help you plan ahead of time where you're going to spend your money. You, in essence, spend it on paper before you actually spend it in real life. This keeps you from making (potentially foolish) impulse purchases. You're also free to enjoy what you do purchase without feeling guilty. Since your spending was part of the plan, it isn't going to keep you from being able to pay the rent next month.

The same principle is true with our time. Although we wouldn't literally plan every minute of it, the goal *is* to plan instead of just letting it happen. What would happen if you started planning with big picture tasks in mind — like when you will work and when you will simply be present with your family? You'll find it much easier to walk away from your work if you're following a plan than if you keep thinking, "I just need to get one more thing done."

As you're developing your plan, realize there will always be something else to do, just like there will always be something else you'd like to buy. The point is that when you spend your time (or money) on paper, you have a clear head to look at *all* your priorities, not only what seems important in the moment.

2. **Plan for the unexpected.**

When someone first learns to budget money, he might set up a plan based on his normal bills and spending habits. This works for a while, but when an unexpected car repair or medical bill shows up, the whole plan can easily derail. An experienced budgeter knows you must plan for the unexpected, setting aside money each month for future car repairs, bills, or surprise expenses. That way, when the unexpected comes, it's not as big of a deal.

It would be wonderful if we could save up extra time for when we need it, but it doesn't quite work that way, does it? Still, we can plan for the unexpected. When we're scheduling our time, we should create margin whenever possible. When the unexpected comes up, we can more easily find time to deal with them. Otherwise, if we fill every minute with activities, we're basically planning to have problems.

3. Roll with the punches.

Wise budgeters know their plan is inevitably going to be derailed, but they don't let that throw them off. Instead, they roll with it. The electric bill was more than we thought? Okay, we'll pull that money from the clothing fund. Car repair cost more than we had saved up? Well, that's why we have an emergency fund.

This same roll-with-the-punches attitude is essential when budgeting our time. Realize life won't always run smoothly. Sometimes, our built-in margin won't cover the speed bumps we cross. When that happens, don't get completely thrown off and give up scheduling altogether. Instead, adjust; tweak your plan, then press on.

4. Get ahead.

Living paycheck to paycheck stinks. So does barely finishing each task the minute before it's due. When you're working on something that has to be done within the hour, your stress level will soar through the roof. But when you're working on a task a week ahead of time, you'll rest easy.

Make it a goal to work ahead whenever possible. Obviously, this is easier said than done, but if you were trying to break the paycheck-to-paycheck cycle financially, you'd tighten up your spending to build up that extra reserve. The same thing is true with your time. If you want to plan ahead, you have to schedule time for that purpose.

5. **Invest in what matters.**

    When we invest money, sometimes it seems like it's not doing anything—it's gone from our account into a nebulous IRA that we'll use in what seems like an eternity. But that investment is important, even if it's not urgent.

    The same is true with our time. We need to invest our time into what truly matters, even if it's not urgent at the time. That means connecting with students, spending time with family, and working to impact eternity.

Journal/Discussion: What budgeting principles do you need to start using for your schedule?

Lesson 17:
Do Not Disturb

Planning or prep periods are supposed to provide time for us to grade papers, plan lessons, and communicate with parents. The sad reality is that these planning periods often are anything but. You know how it is. You've had a crazy day. The kids walk out the door, and you sit down to finally get something done. You check your email and find a complaint from a parent. When you finally resolve the issue, half your time is up, and you haven't checked anything off your list. So you determine to buckle down and get going. Then a student comes in to ask you a quick question.

Five minutes later, you dive back in, only to be distracted by a funny text from your friend. It's been a tough day and you needed a laugh, so you smile, respond to the text, and then return to your papers. You grade the first one and "Ding!" the bell rings and kids start pouring back in your room. You sigh and stand up. You worked the whole period, but you didn't get anything done.

Sound familiar? Distractions are a natural part of teaching, but despite them— maybe because of them — we must create focused work times that allow us to actually get chunks of work done at school. Not every planning period will be a focused work time, but you should create at least a few of these per week. Before you say that's impossible, here are specific ways to reduce the distractions and disruptions.

Reducing Disruptions During your Planning Periods

1. **Make appointments with yourself and guard that time.** If you had an appointment to meet with a parent, you would respect that commitment and deny any other requests to meet with you during that time. The same should be true when you set appointments with yourself. When you plan a dedicated work period and someone asks to stop by to talk with you, tell them you have a prior obligation. This is not a lie because you've made a prior obligation with yourself. You'll be amazed how satisfying it feels to guard this time, and your colleagues can always stop by later.

2. **Don't check your email.** When you check your email, you're distracted by requests for your time. Instead, keep your email closed except for a designated time (or two) each day when you plan to reply to emails.

3. **Turn off your notifications.** Notifications are distracting. Turning them off is freeing. Keep notifications only for your most essential forms of communication and turn everything else off. Check them when you want, but don't let them disrupt your day.

4. **Use airplane mode.** If calls and texts are a big disruption for you, airplane mode allows you to declare yourself unavailable for a few minutes. And don't worry, those texts will be there when you come back.

5. **Use software to block distractions.** Programs like Freedom (**www.freedom.to**) allow you to block certain websites during

focused work time. If you find yourself wasting too much precious time scrolling through social media, this is for you.

6. **Shut your classroom door.** Consider posting a sign that says, "Teacher working. Please come back later." You can't do this every day, but when you need to get something done, it's okay to tell people this isn't a good time.

7. **Have designated times students can (and cannot) come ask you questions.** If you're bombarded with student questions during work times, try planning more strategically. Set certain times or days when students can ask you questions and explain that they need to respect your time and stick to these office hours. Or, teach them that when the sign is outside, they need to come back later. It's healthy to draw these boundaries.

8. **Find a secluded spot to work.** Sometimes you have to get out of your room. Is there a part of your building that no one goes to? Maybe camp out there for a bit. If you have a large block of time, consider getting off campus. You might marvel at how much you can get done in an hour at the library.

9. **Do "errands" at the end of the planning period instead of the beginning.** If you need to run copies, stop by the office, or talk to a student, save those tasks for the end of the period, not the beginning. The knowledge that the bell's about to ring will keep that five-minute task from consuming 10, 15, 20 minutes—like it easily does if you run errands at the start of the period.

Journal/Discussion: What helps you stay focused during planning periods? What do you want to do differently?

Lesson 18:
I Can't Think

You sit down at your desk after a long day, glad to *finally* have a few minutes to tackle your overflowing to-do list. As usual, your mind is racing:

Let's see, I need to write next week's lesson plans, grade math tests, call Jeremy's mom, talk to Mr. Edwards, record this stack of homework, and clean my room.

So where do you start? Your list is overwhelming, so you think, *I'll just check my email first and then tackle...something.*

Your email inbox reveals four new messages that need your response. You answer them and feel a small sense of accomplishment that you got back to parents so quickly. But now you're once again staring at that to-do list.

Ugh, I'll never get this all done. I do need to call Jeremy's mom, so I guess I'll get that over with.

Ten minutes and one phone call later you realize you *must* get to those lesson plans. So you grab your books, open your laptop, and start to type. There's just one problem.

You can't think.

Try as you might, you can't seem to keep your classes straight—or remember that perfect idea you had yesterday. Your mind is blank—or maybe it's overflowing. And instead of busting out those lesson plans you spend your last thirty minutes waiting for inspiration. Finally, you give up and shut your computer.

Guess I'll try again tomorrow.

When we think about ending the stress cycle and finding balance, we tend to focus on managing our time. But if we want to stop feeling so overwhelmed, we must also manage our focus, or our mental energy.

When we finally get a few minutes to work, we need to focus and accomplish something. We can't afford to get nothing done because we've used up all our mental energy trying to decide what to do.

Our minds have enough to worry about without constantly figuring out what task we should tackle next. When we develop a system that helps us keep track of our tasks and organize them in a simple way, we free up our mental energy for the things we need our creative brainpower for—like coming up with engaging lesson plans. When our minds are more focused (and less burnt out), we accomplish more in less time, and we feel energized, too.

Let's take a look at a step-by-step plan to manage our overtaxed focus and free up some mental energy for when we need it most.

Managing Our Mental Focus

Step 1: Develop a start-of-day and end-of-day routine.

If you always complete the same list of activities when you arrive at school and another list before you leave, you will accomplish many of your responsibilities without even having to think about them. Here's an example of what your routine might look like:

Start of Day: Check mailbox, write bellwork on the board, write homework on the board, prepare supplies, review lesson plans, check email (time permitting)

End of Day: Process all late/absent work that was turned in, record grades from daily homework and classwork, empty paperwork in-bin, clean up desk (i.e. make the piles look semi-organized), tidy up room, check to-do list, check mailbox

The point isn't to completely finish these routines one hundred percent of the time. We are teachers, which means we're going to be interrupted. But if you develop these routines, you're going to accomplish these tasks way more often and way more efficiently.

Next Step: Think about the things you currently do at the start and end of your school day. Are these tasks the best use of this precious time? Are there other things you should be doing every day? Write down a tentative start-of-day and end-of-day routine. Then adjust it over the next few weeks until you've fine-tuned an effective routine.

Step 2: Write down all the things you need to do.

We often treat our brains like a filing cabinet, stuffing all the information we can in there (including all the random things we need to do) and hoping we can remember it all. But when we try to keep our to-do lists in our heads, we feel ultra-stressed, and it's no wonder why. We're spending so much of our mental energy trying to keep track of all our tasks that there's no mental space left to accomplish any of them.

The second we write down a to-do list, our minds are free. Yes, we still have to actually do all the tasks; but they're written down, and we no longer have to worry about remembering them.

Next step: Write down every task you need to accomplish. Whether it's for school or home, whether it's due now, next week, or five months from now — jot it down. Get everything out on paper so you don't have to carry it all around in your mind.

Journal/Put it Into Practice: Complete both of the *next steps* listed above. Then come back tomorrow for the final three steps.

Lesson 19:
I Heart Procrastination

In the last chapter, we learned the first two steps to managing our focus: creating start-of-day and end-of-day routines, and keeping a detailed to-do list.

But if the mental to-do list will destroy your focus, its cousin, the mile-long to-do list, will kill your motivation. You know what I'm talking about. You sit down for your planning period and pick up your to-do list only to be reminded that there are literally thirty-one things you need to do. Your mind panics (just a bit) as you frantically try to figure out which of these tasks you should tackle first.

Clearly, we need a few more steps if we're going to free up our focus:

Step 3: Intentionally procrastinate.

When we're staring at thirty-one tasks our brains tend to get a bit overwhelmed. But if we say, "I don't need to worry about these six items till next month, these twelve are for next week, and these nine can be done on Thursday or Friday," then suddenly we only have four items left to do today. And that, my friend, is powerful.

Too often we say, "Here's my to-do list. I'm going to cross off as many things as I can today." But, honestly, this approach doesn't work that well. We aren't motivated because there's no clear finish line. And no matter how many things we cross off the list, we feel bad about what we didn't finish instead of feeling good about what we did. What do you think that does to our productivity, much less our stress level?

Try changing it up. Put only a few essential items on your daily to-do list. You'll probably find yourself actually accomplishing all or most of them, feeling a whole lot better about your day, and—best of all—not feeling so stressed about the items you've intentionally left for another day.

Next step: Get the Intentional Procrastination To-Do List System (including printable to-do lists) in the bonus resource pack at teach4theheart.com/TakeHeartBonus.

This system will help you separate your to-do list into separate lists. You'll make one (short) list for today and put everything else under one of the following categories: tomorrow, this week, this month, next month, and this year. Then, make it part of your daily routine (either end-of-day or start-of-day) to choose the next day's to-do's. Only choose a few vital to-do items that you can realistically finish during the day.

Finally, don't you dare put too many things on your list because you're worried you'll finish everything early and then waste time. If you finish early, maybe you deserve to actually go home on time. But if you want to keep working, you can grab an item from tomorrow's to-do list. Then you'll actually be ahead! Bottom line—don't put items on your "today" list because you hope you can get to them. Only write a few things you can realistically get done today—assuming a big problem doesn't derail you (because we know that never happens ☺).

Step 4: Designate certain tasks for specific days of the week. The more we can organize and pre-determine when we'll do certain tasks, the less mental energy we spend trying to figure out when we'll fit them in. One powerful strategy is to designate certain tasks for certain days of the week.

Here's an example: I recently found myself resenting many of my household responsibilities such as paying bills, dealing with insurance claims, or ordering a new smoke detector. I could never seem to find time for them and felt like they were intruding into the rest of my to-do list. I was getting more and more frustrated, so I decided to designate Friday afternoons to work on household responsibilities. Suddenly, they're no longer a frustration. When my husband asks if I can call about our slow internet, instead of grumbling because, "When on earth am I gonna do that?" I just think, "No problem. I'll do it Friday."

Now it's your turn. What tasks always feel like interruptions? What items do you never seem to find time for, even though they have to get done? Try designating a certain day for them. For example, you could say, "I'm going to do all my non-urgent parent communication Thursday after school." Then, any time you think, "I should probably update Emma's mom about her science test," instead of stressing about when on earth you're going to do that, write it on your Thursday list. On Thursday, knock out all your emails and phone calls at once.

Other examples of tasks you might consider grouping are:

- printing/copying
- lesson planning (designate 1-3 days a week where they are your focus)
- grading catch-up (Do NOT save all your grading for one day, but designate a time to catch up on major grading if you're behind.)
- student conferences
- filing
- room décor/bulletin boards/clean-up

Next step: Identify tasks you can designate for certain days of the week. If possible, consider theming each day. For example:

Monday – grading catch-up

Tuesday – lesson plans

Wednesday – lesson plans

Thursday – parent and student communication

Friday – printing/copying

(Please note that this wouldn't be the only thing you did that day, but it *would* be a major theme for the day.)

Step 5: Designate and guard your off hours.

If you want to lower your stress and keep your focus, you have to take time off. You must set boundaries around your time and choose when you will stop working. You may need hard lines like, "I will leave school by 4:15" or "I will only work for one hour this evening." Don't be afraid to use a timer and to ask your spouse or friend to keep you accountable.

Time off is essential, but for the time to be sufficiently refreshing, your mind needs a break, too. That means no talking about work and no thinking about work. None at all. This idea was revolutionary to me at first. *You mean I shouldn't be thinking about work all the time? But when am I going to come up with solutions to all these problems?*

Here's the truth: Yes, we can (and probably should) use *some* of our off hours to brainstorm about teaching, but we also desperately need time that is truly off. Time where we refuse to think about work and let our minds wander elsewhere. Time to let our minds refresh and rejuvenate. You'll be amazed how less ominous Monday morning feels when you've let your mind refresh over the weekend.

Next step: Determine clear boundaries for when you will and will not work. Then, give yourself permission to stop thinking about school when you're off. When a school issue comes to mind during off-hours, decide to either think about it or let your mind refresh. (Keep in mind that you can't do both.)

Journal/Put it into Practice: Complete the *next steps* listed above.

Lesson 20:
A Bag Full of Bricks

She felt like she was lugging home a bag full of bricks. In reality, it was three lesson plan binders, two textbooks, and about countless hours-worth of grading. No, this wasn't an abnormal day. Tracy always hauled her teacher bag home — a bag full of papers she knew she would never actually finish.

But that's just part of teaching, right? Par for the course. Our work follows us home then follows us back to work, and we're never free of it. We practically live in a perpetual stress cycle that we have to survive until summer rolls around. Then, and only then, we can finally breathe again. That's the only way to be an effective teacher, right?

Maybe not. Tracy used to think that overflowing teacher bag of hers was somehow essential to her success as a teacher. She doesn't think that anymore. In fact, she's realized that teaching does not have to be an endless struggle of stress, being overwhelmed, and exhaustion. Tracy learned how to control her work hours through lessons she learned from Angela Watson's 40 Hour Teacher Workweek Club. She found some balance in her life, and she was still able to be an effective teacher.

The 40 Hour Teacher Workweek Club is chock-full of incredible time-saving techniques—way more than we could ever cover in one book, much less in one chapter. But there are six over-arching principles that form the foundation of the club and can be applied to all areas of teaching and life.

6 Keys to Getting More Done in Less Time

1. **Eliminate unintentional breaks.**

   The goal is not to eliminate *all* breaks, but to work when you plan to work and break when you plan to break. During work times, don't allow yourself to be distracted by social media, your phones, your own (non-intentional) procrastination, or anything else.

2. **Figure out the main thing, and do it first.**

   This concept has transformed my productivity, and it can do wonders for yours, too. Each day, decide what one task most needs to be done that day. Then during the first block of time you get, tackle the main thing *first*. Don't check your email or throw some grades in the computer first. Instead, complete the most important task, *and then* worry about everything else. You'll feel relieved knowing that even if the rest of the day comes unglued, you got your most crucial task done.

3. **Work ahead by batching, and avoid multi-tasking unless the work is mindless.**

   Batching means doing similar tasks together instead of spreading them out. For example, if you make all your copies for the whole week at once, that saves time over running to the copier five times a day. Getting ahead by batching takes planning, but it feels wonderful once it's done.

Now when it comes to multi-tasking, I am a chronic multi-tasker, and maybe you are, too. But multi-tasking only helps when the work is truly mindless (things like cleaning your room or making copies). Otherwise, multi-tasking actually breaks your focus and makes you less efficient.

4. **Look for innovative ways to relax any standards that create unnecessary work.**

Sometimes we make up standards for ourselves that are unnecessarily high. We decide in our minds that this is the way it has to be done, even though it's taking up a ton of time. But do we have to do it that way? There's probably another method that will work just as well in a lot less time.

The key to letting go of unnecessary standards is to remember that when we say *yes* to one thing, we're saying *no* to something else that might be even more important. Ask yourself if your own standards are truly worth the time or if there's an innovative way to relax this unnecessary standard.

5. **Use scheduling to create boundaries around your time.**

If you don't plan when you're going to work and when you're not, work will always spill over into your family life. But if you instead decide when you're going to work and schedule that time, you create boundaries around your time, and you're able to walk away.

6. **Always look for small ways to save time. They add up.**

Don't ever discount ways to save five minutes here or ten minutes there. These little changes add up to big results and give you the freedom you desperately need.

Remember Tracy, lugging home her all-too-familiar teacher bag of bricks? Well, that was before Tracy implemented these strategies from Angela Watson's 40 Hour Teacher Workweek Club. When she did, she ditched her overflowing teacher bag and hasn't taken grading home in over four months. And what's better—she's still getting everything done **at school** in about 43 hours a week.

I wish I could share everything she learned, but there's so much incredible info in the club that I couldn't even fit it into its own book. You can find out more about the club, however, at **www.teach4theheart.com/40hourteacher**.

Journal/Discussion: **Which of these strategies do you most want to implement in the coming weeks? What's one change you can make right now.**

Lesson 21:
Where the Rubber Meets the Road

We've established that balance matters; we've discovered key principles to manage your time and focus. But we can't leave this section without giving some specific time-saving tips, tips that can save you time starting tomorrow.

1. **Don't grade everything.**

   If you are grading every piece of work your students do, stop! This is too overwhelming and takes too much time. Instead, tell your students that any piece of work they do *could* be taken for a grade but only actually grade it occasionally. That way, they have the incentive to always try their best, but you're not buried in paperwork.

2. **Give the impression you grade more than you do.**

   Whether or not you're going to grade something, collect the papers anyhow. For those you're not grading, either put them directly into your outbox, or flip through them and put check marks and smiley faces on the ones that look good at a glance. This takes about one minute and makes the students feel that their work is being noticed and valued.

3. **Take advantage of a few minutes here and a few minutes there.**

   When you have three minutes here or even thirty seconds there, use them to get something done. Grade a few papers, scratch an item off your to-do list, or do some mental planning. While spare minutes here and there don't seem like much, they add up. You can probably grade stacks of papers during the day just by claiming these unused minutes, and using this time wisely can be the difference between going home empty-handed or with an over-flowing bag. Keep a stack of papers by your podium and when there's a lull in teaching, grade. (Just make sure the lull is because kids are working. We all know an actual lull will quickly result in disaster.)

4. **Learn to type faster.**

   You probably don't have time in the middle of the school year, but if you're a slow or even average typist, put this on your summer to-do list. Typing quickly will save you a ton of time. Writing lesson plans, crafting emails, creating worksheets, and entering grades all require typing, and the faster you can type, the faster these tasks get done. Learning to type faster will be a worthwhile investment of your time, and you can easily find free typing programs online.

5. **Forgo elaborate decorations and visuals** (at least for now).

   If you're spending hours crafting the perfect bulletin board or an elaborate helpers chart, it's time for a paradigm switch. These things are flashy and showy, but they don't help your students learn any better. You can make your classroom fun and colorful without spending hours on the decorations. Think pre-made posters and student work.

When I was in college, I learned how to create classroom graphics by blowing up a picture with an overhead, tracing it with permanent marker, and coloring it in with multi-colored chalk. One graphic literally took hours and hours. In the real world, there's not time for this — at least not if you're taking a bunch of work home. If you love this side of teaching, then keep it as part of your day, but consider scaling back until you get your time more under control.

6. **Focus on efficiency, not speed.**

   When you rush to get a task done quickly, you make mistakes. Then you have to go back and correct them. You end up not saving time at all. In fact, you often end up taking longer. Instead, focus on efficiency. Have a stack of grading? Try to be efficient—that means working at your maximum productivity. Be focused and don't get distracted. Work to the best of your ability, but don't rush.

7. **Grade homework and classwork as quickly as possible.**

   You already know not to grade everything, but when you do grade classwork or homework (smaller grades), make the grading as easy as possible. Have your students grade each others' homework in class and put a question mark if they are not sure or think someone graded their paper wrong. Don't take time to re-grade the whole paper if there isn't a question mark. Write the grade and move on.

   Other grades will be worth spending more time on. As an algebra teacher, I spent hours going through individual problems on tests and quizzes to award partial credit. This was time-consuming but worth the effort. The key is to prioritize. Determine what is worth the time and what needs a quick grade.

8. Ditch the rubrics.

Get creative with grading sheets for writing projects or other subjective grading. Using a checklist grading sheet instead of a rubric saves time. Instead of doing the math then finagle the numbers so they add up to the grade you know it should be, a checklist grading sheet simply lists all the things you expect of students. You can easily circle everything that is incorrect or subpar and put a check mark or smiley face by everything they did well. Either assign a holistic grade or take off a certain number of points for each circle. Not having to do the math saves time, and the circles and checks justify the grade (while also keeping you from having to write a million comments). See Appendix C for an example checklist grading form. An editable form is also available in the bonus pack at **Teach4theHeart.com/TakeHeartBonus**.

9. Keep track of your lesson plans from year to year.

When you teach a new course or have a new curriculum, everything is more time consuming. But taking a few minutes to track what you're doing this year, what's working well, and what's not, will more than pay off. If you have all your notes in one place at the end of the year, you'll thank yourself a million times over when you don't have to reinvent the wheel next year.

10. Organize your files (both physical and digital).

You don't have to be uber-organized (my storage closet was a bit of a mess), but the things you use most often—the files you always need to access—those need to be organized so you don't waste time searching high and low for something that should be right there. On your computer, don't keep every document you've ever made in "My Documents." Instead, have a folder for each course, then within that course, a folder for each chapter. Make things easy to find so that you're not searching and searching and ... searching.

Journal/Discussion: Which time-saving technique(s) do you want to start implementing?

Lesson 22:
But Wait, There's More!

Still looking for more timesaving tips? Got you covered.

11. Pray for clarity and efficiency.

Without God, we can do nothing. He is our strength, our
help, and our rest. He can and will give us clarity and help us
work more efficiently. And if we're listening, He'll also help us
balance our lists of tasks with our greater purpose: helping our
students.

12. Master copy and paste.

When writing lesson plans, crafting emails, or developing
assessments, get in the habit of asking yourself, "Did I already
create something similar?" If so, find it, copy, paste, and
then tweak. This is especially helpful with emails. How many
times have you emailed a parent about a student not doing
his homework? Craft a generic email template and save a
copy. Then, when you need to email a parent, start with the
template and customize it to fit the situation.

13. Get help from your students.

Student helpers are not just for primary grades. Are you
responsible to clean your room? Use the last minute of class

to have your students pick up trash. Students also like to help with various classroom tasks like organizing papers, decorating a bulletin board, or sharpening pencils.

14. Enlist help from parents, teachers' aides, friends, and family.

Students can be a huge help, but there's some things they can't do—like grade their own tests. For more advanced tasks, enlist help and invest time training them. At first, you'll worry you're spending more time explaining than you would by doing it yourself. But once they learn your system, they'll be able to do it without your help and you will save tons of time by simply passing off tasks to them.

15. Use online resources, but don't browse indefinitely.

Online worksheets and websites can save time, but browsing the web for the perfect worksheet can end up taking longer than creating one yourself. My strategy is to have a few go-to sites that have outstanding activities. When I need one, I check those, but if they don't have what I want, I make my own. (A *quick* Google search might be okay, but you know how quickly a *quick* search becomes a *long* search. Consider setting a timer.)

16. Avoid social media during school hours.

The Facebook vortex has derailed more than its share of prep periods. Social media can be a treasure trove of classroom ideas, but consider saving them for when you're home—or at least until your big to-do's are done for the day. While you're at work, get all the tasks done that feel like work. When you're at home, relax on the couch with Pinterest or your favorite Facebook teachers' group.

17. Find an efficient way to deal with absent work requests.

Absent work requests can make a big dent in your time, especially when the flu's going around. Design an efficient way of dealing with them—a way that will take you the least amount of time possible. For me, my simplified week-long lesson plans fit on a single sheet of paper and include homework, tests, quizzes, and an overview of the topics we covered. I simply hit print and staple it to the request form, attach any necessary worksheets, and I'm done. Or, I copy and paste it into an email. This may not work with your system, but find something that does — something fast and efficient.

18. Get up a little earlier.

I can hear the groaning. *Get up earlier? Are you kidding me? I'm already up at the crack of dawn!* I hear you, but a few extra minutes in the morning when you're fresh can save you an hour of work in the evening. For many, the morning time is that much more productive. So when your alarm clock goes off early and you want to hit snooze, imagine yourself relaxing on your couch that evening or getting to go to bed early.

19. Don't promise to send regular reports to parents
(unless your administration requires you to do so).

Not only does this take time, but if you forget even once, you've broken your promise. Instead, when parents ask for regular reports, ask them to email or call you, and tell them you'll be happy to respond. This puts the responsibility back where it belongs—with the parents. And you only have to hit reply to the emails that come, instead of trying to remember to send them.

20. Send bulk emails when appropriate.

Bulk emails help us communicate quickly and efficiently. They're much faster than printing and passing out forms, and more parents actually see them. Bulk emails can be used for more than announcements. Are there eight kids who didn't turn in their projects? Instead of contacting each one individually, send one email to all of them, putting the email addresses in the BCC field so parents won't see who else got the email.

P.S. Do not do this all the time. Often we need to write a more personalized email or even pick up the phone. But using bulk emails when it is appropriate will free up time for when you need to be more detailed.

21. Don't agonize over the possibility of a typo in emails.

We want to be accurate and professional in all our interactions, but it's not worth your time to scour your emails over and over in search of an elusive typo. Typos happen. They are part of life. Parents understand. There shouldn't be a ton of them, but an occasional typo is going to slip through, and it's not worth your time to read each email six times just in case.

22. Don't double-check your grading key.

When you write your own test, don't bother to double-check your answer key, especially for math problems. Instead, grade your best student's test first, and check any answers they appear to get wrong. You should catch mistakes easily—and it will take much less time than reworking each problem.

23. Learn how to better use your computer.

If you're not comfortable with your computer, do yourself a favor by learning how to use it more efficiently. Consider taking a computer class over the summer or asking a more tech-savvy colleague for some tips. The better you know how to use your computer, the more efficient you'll be, and the more time you'll save.

Here's my favorite time-saving computer tip: The more you can stick to the keyboard, as opposed to switching from keyboard to mouse, the faster you can work. To switch from window to window (for example, from the internet to Word), hold Alt and hit Tab on a PC or hold Command and hit Tab on a Mac. You can then tab through all your open windows. Pretty cool, huh?

24. Take time to get to the root of the problem.

This may sound like the opposite of a time-saving tip, but investing in solving issues now will save you time in the long run. When dealing with parents, students, or even fellow educators, take time to discover and discuss the real issues. Then you can actually make progress towards resolving issues instead of uselessly repeating the same conversation over and over.

Journal/Discussion: What are your favorite time-saving tips? What do you want to change to save more time?

Lesson 23:
Praying for Balance

I hope you've found helpful time-saving strategies and are developing balance-minded thinking. But, once again, we cannot neglect prayer.

God designed us, placed us where we are, and wants to work in and through us each day to accomplish His purposes. Doesn't He care how we spend our time? Isn't He able to guard our calendars and help us correctly order our priorities?

Take heart. The answer is a resounding *Yes!*

As we strive for balance, let's always turn to the One who knows, cares, and can do exceedingly above all that we ask or think according to the power that works in us.

Take a few minutes to pray right now.

Journal/Put it into Practice: Pray about the struggles you've been facing with balance, priorities, and time-management. You may want to pray for the following:

- That God would help you use your time wisely and to know how to care for both your students and your family

- That God would give you strength and energy to do His work today

- That God would guide you as you guard your calendar, showing you when to say *yes* and when to say *no*

Resources

Check out these resources for more help finding balance:

FREE Guide: How to Work a Reasonable Number of Hours as a Teacher

My friend Angela Watson has created a guide to help you choose a reasonable number of hours to work and then stick to it. She's graciously offering it to *Take Heart and Teach* readers for free at **www.teach4theheart.com/balance**.

Angela Watson's 40 Hour Teacher Workweek Club

The 40 Hour Teacher Workweek Club is helping thousands of teachers cut 3, 5, even 10+ hours off their workweek (the average time saved is 11 hours a week!) It's not about teaching 40 hours per se but about finding a way to teach that is sustainable.

Find out more at **www.teach4theheart.com/40hourteacher**.

Part 3:
Take Heart and Teach with Joy

Be anxious for nothing, but in everything by prayer and supplication, with thanksgiving, let your requests be made known to God; and the peace of God, which surpasses all understanding, will guard your hearts and minds through Christ Jesus. –Phiippians 4:6-7

The challenges of teaching can leave us frustrated and stressed. But take heart; this isn't the way God intended us to live.

God wants us to teach with joy, peace, and (yes it's possible) rest, even when things are going wrong. Let's discover how to thrive amidst the challenges of teaching, becoming a shining light for Him in the process.

Lesson 24:
An Audience of One

Piles of grading. Irate parents. Disrespectful, disinterested students. Constant testing and unreasonable requirements. These things, and many more, conspire against us, working to bring us down. They discourage us; they make us wonder if we are wasting our time.

Throughout this section of the book, we'll discuss how to handle discouragement and frustration, returning us to a place where we are once again passionate and engaged in our teaching. But here's the first question: When we are discouraged, frustrated, or feeling down, where do we go for encouragement? Do we dig deep within ourselves to find strength? Do we console ourselves with thoughts of past students whom we've been able to impact? Do we hop on the Internet and search for inspirational messages and encouragement that we can do it? These things might help for a time, but their pick-me-up effect doesn't last.

What we need is more of God. He alone can bring us unshakeable joy, peace, and rest—despite whatever challenges or circumstances we are facing. And He is the one we must seek to please with our teaching. When we feel no one notices, we must remember that God sees the long hours and the shed tears. He knows our biggest frustrations and our deepest hurts. He doesn't overlook us, and He doesn't take us for granted.

And whatever you do, do it heartily, as to the Lord and not to men, knowing that from the Lord you will receive the reward of the inheritance; for you serve the Lord Christ. —Colossians 3:23-24

Colossians 3:23-24 reminds us that we are working for an audience of One: our Lord Jesus Christ. When no one else seems to notice, He sees. When no one else seems to care, He cares. When our words seem to be falling flat, He sees our effort and is pleased with our faithfulness.

So, in the midst of the busyness, the frustration, and the chaos, take a moment and remember the real reason that you are teaching. It shouldn't be for the praise. It shouldn't be for the satisfaction. It shouldn't even be for the kids. The real reason we are teaching should be to please and honor God.

If we keep our focus on Him, what's happening around us won't matter as much. When we depend on Him, He gives us strength, endurance, and perspective to keep going and truly make a difference in our students' hearts and lives.

Therefore, my beloved brethren, be steadfast, immovable, always abounding in the work of the Lord, knowing that your labor is not in vain in the Lord. —I Corinthians 15:58

Journal/Discussion: When you're struggling, do you tend to look to yourself or God? What needs to change in your perspective?

Lesson 25:
Gotta' Be God

Teaching can be a roller coaster ride of emotions. The ups and downs are innumerable, and mountaintop days are often followed by incredibly challenging ones. But whether we enjoy our time teaching or wallow in misery doesn't depend on what's happening around us. Our joy (or lack thereof) depends on our attitude, our choices, and our walk with God.

In these next three sections, we'll examine eight problems that lead to discouragement and the solutions to overcome them.

PROBLEM #1: You're trying to be a better teacher on your own (or "with God's help")

As teachers, we're used to figuring out how to make things work. But if we're not careful, we'll try to teach, inspire, motivate, and even prick our students' consciences in our own strength instead of relying on God to make us what we need to be.

Or maybe you've realized you desperately need God, so you try to be a good teacher "with God's help." But listen to that statement for a minute. It sure sounds like it's still **you** trying to do it—and you're tacking on God's help like you'd add a few bonus points to a test.

This doesn't work. How many times have you tried to somehow do better and failed? Determined not to lose your patience with your students, only to find yourself yelling the next day? Endeavored to stop complaining or gossiping only to fall into it again? Worked on having a respectful attitude towards a difficult administrator, only to remain constantly frustrated by them?

It's just not working, is it? Furthermore, self-reliance is not the message of the Gospel. Jesus didn't come only to save us from sin's penalty and then "help us" struggle through life. He wants to change us from the inside out—to work His work in us, to produce His fruit. So, what are we missing?

THE SOLUTION: Realize God must do the work in and through us.

Listen to these verses:

Abide in Me, and I in you. As the branch cannot bear fruit of itself, unless it abides in the vine, neither can you, unless you abide in Me. I am the vine, you are the branches. He who abides in Me, and I in him, bears much fruit; for without Me you can do nothing... These things I have spoken to you, that My joy may remain in you, and that your joy may be full. –John 15:4-5, 11

For it is God who works in you both to will and to do for His good pleasure. –Philippians 2:13

God Himself must do the work in us, changing us from the inside out and producing His fruit of love, joy, peace, patience, and more. This mindset shift is subtle but powerful. Stop trying to be better. Stop trying to do better on your own. Cry out to God and ask Him to change you. He is the Potter and has obligated Himself to mold us if we simply trust and surrender to Him. Which brings us to the next problem:

PROBLEM #2: You're not *really* trusting God.

In any challenge we face, whether it is a difficult administrator, a frustrating co-worker, a scary evaluation, an over-reaching parent, an overwhelming stack of paperwork, or even a dreaded class (from you-know-where), our souls can immediately be at peace if we choose to trust God.

The problem is that we don't actually trust Him. Not really. We may say that we do, but our stress and worry reveal otherwise. If we truly trusted God, we would rest in His plan and surrender to whatever He has for our lives, including this uncomfortable challenge we're currently facing.

Instead, we worry about God's plan, fearing that what He has for us may not be what we want. We secretly wonder if God might have gotten it wrong this time, or we speculate that this situation is so bad that maybe, just maybe, He's not actually in control.

But when we say that out loud, we see how ridiculous it is, right? God's plans are always best. He is never wrong. And He is always in control.

THE SOLUTION: Choose to trust God, surrender to His plan, and leave your worry with Him.

Often, we bring our burdens to Christ in prayer but then immediately pick them up and try to carry them ourselves the second we say, "Amen." But what if we left them at His feet? What if we fully trusted Him to take care of our concerns? What if the next time you were worried about your observation or your testing results, you took the issue to God in prayer and left your worry with Him, refusing to stress about it any longer? Yes, you'd still need to do the necessary prep work, but you wouldn't have to carry the burden any longer.

You'd finally experience the incredible peace described in Philippians 4:6-7: "Be anxious for nothing, but in everything by prayer and supplication, with thanksgiving, let your requests be made known to God; and the peace of God, which surpasses all understanding, will guard your hearts and minds through Christ Jesus. "

Journal/Discussion: Which of these two problems do you recognize most in yourself? What do you need to do differently?

P.S. If you think all this is easier said than done, I get it. But it's also easier than you might think. We'd love for you to join us in Teach Uplifted, where we explore all the ins and outs of what it means to trust God—and how to actually do it on a daily basis. You can get more info at **www.teachuplifted.com**.

Lesson 26:
New Thoughts, New Joy

To teach with joy we must first depend on God and trust Him implicitly. But that's not enough. We must also allow what we believe to change the way we view our circumstances. Let's examine two more problems that can lead to discouragement and how to overcome them with God's truths.

PROBLEM #3: You're thinking untrue thoughts.

We can't always change our situations, but we can always choose how we think about them. The problem is that we often don't realize how unbiblical (and therefore untrue) our thought patterns are. We don't realize the grave damage these thoughts are doing.

For example, do you recognize any of these common thoughts?

"I don't deserve to be treated like this?"

"I'm not good enough. I can't do this."

"I shouldn't have to deal with this."

Despite how often we hear these phrases or even think them ourselves, all of them are decidedly unbiblical. And what's more, they'll leave you continually frustrated and discouraged. So what do we do?

SOLUTION: Renew your mind by taking every thought captive.

Casting down arguments and every high thing that exalts itself against the knowledge of God, bringing every thought into captivity to the obedience of Christ. –2 Corinthians 10:5

And do not be conformed to this world, but be transformed by the renewing of your mind, that you may prove what is that good and acceptable and perfect will of God. –Romans 12:2

You can learn to take your thoughts captive and renew your mind with Biblical thinking. When you're feeling discouraged, first pray and yield yourself to Christ. Then, analyze your thinking. Ask yourself why you're *really* upset. Often, there's a hidden reason such as our own pride or unrealized expectations.

Next, think about the Biblical truth that will address your feelings. For example, if you've been treated unfairly by an administrator and have been telling yourself you don't deserve to be treated like that, you might realize this frustration is caused by pride and the desire to be respected. Since pride is abhorrent to God, it must always be cast down and replaced with genuine humility (James 4:6). Furthermore, you don't work for your administrators. You work for God (Colossians 3:23-24). So instead of choosing to worry about what your administrator or anyone else thinks of you, you must choose to remember that God's approval is all that matters. Determine to do your best, but leave the results up to Him.

Once you've identified wrong thinking and replaced it with Biblical truth, choose to believe that truth. Then, change your thoughts regarding the situation, maybe even writing them down. Tell yourself the truth whenever your old thought patterns surface.

Keep reminding yourself over and over until the old fades and the new becomes second nature.

Get these steps in a printable worksheet in the bonus pack at **Teach4theHeart.com/TakeHeartBonus**.

PROBLEM #4: You're assuming the worst.

Few things tend to frustrate us more than those around us. Whether it's an out-of-touch administrator, helicopter parent, unmotivated colleague, or challenging student, there is always someone clawing to get under our skin.

Here's the thing: Often the frustration we feel towards this person is a result of our assuming the worst. We might think, *they just don't like me.* Or we question their behavior because we can't imagine any reason to justify it. Maybe we see how they react to us, so we wonder, *they treated me like that, I can't imagine the horrible things they must say to their students!*

But what if instead of judging them or their situation, we gave them the benefit of the doubt? What if we realized there is probably more to the story? What if we considered that they might be going through challenges of their own that are affecting how they handle their day-to-day problems? What if, instead of letting our own frustrations rise in righteous indignation, we chose to shower them with grace?

SOLUTION: Give grace and the benefit of the doubt.

When God's Spirit is working in and through us, we can hold others in high esteem regardless of what they do. We can remember that God loves them and that we fall short too. We can extend grace, as we would want others to do for us.

As we give grace to others, we find that our own joy is renewed. As we stop worrying and fretting about everyone else, we find God's peace and love filling our own hearts, and our discouragement and frustration melts away.

Journal/Discussion: What thoughts do you need to take captive? Who do you need to choose to give grace to?

Lesson 27:
A Moment to Breathe

In our quest to banish discouragement, we first determined to rely on God and trust Him no matter what. Then we chose to take our thoughts captive and give grace to others. But there are four *practical* problems that could still derail us.

PROBLEM #5: You're exhausted.

While complex spiritual or emotional issues are often at the root of our discouragement, sometimes the answer is way simpler—we're exhausted. When we're running on empty, everything is harder to deal with. And if we keep going, our bodies, minds, and even our spirits take the toll.

Too often we laugh off our physical needs of rest, good nutrition, and exercise. *I don't have time for that!* We consider ourselves martyrs by "putting our students first." But we're not helping our students when we're so tired we can hardly think straight. We do them no service when we snap at them because we lack the patience or energy to deal with their shenanigans. We aren't putting them first when we subject them to crazy mood swings due to our poor eating choices, or when we simply can't muster the passion to teach effective lessons.

If this sounds familiar, stop fooling yourself. You're not helping your students. You're certainly not helping you. Your energy needs to be your priority. Starting now.

SOLUTION: Increase your energy by getting more rest, eating better, drinking more water and/or exercising.

Sounds impossible? Okay, one step at a time. What's *one change* you could make right now? Today. Do you need to go to bed earlier? Most of us can do that if we simply choose to.

How about adding a 20-minute nap into your schedule? (I may or may not have napped in my closet during a free hour on particularly tiring days.) Maybe you could bring a water bottle from home so you drink more water throughout the day, or make time for a 20-minute walk three days a week.

You don't have to change everything overnight, but you must choose to start making your well-being a priority.

PROBLEM #6: You're trying to do everything.

If your schedule is jam-packed with meetings, responsibilities, to-do's, and activities, with no empty space to rest and refresh, it's no wonder you're overwhelmed and discouraged. Yes, teaching is a fast-paced, busy career path, but it doesn't have to take over your life.

Too many of you are taking on too many responsibilities. You're saying *yes* to every request made to you out of guilt, obligation, or maybe even a genuine desire to make a difference. But, regardless, you're missing a key principle: when you agree to one thing, you sacrifice something else. This is simple logic. When you accept one responsibility you automatically give it time and energy that can no longer be used for something else.

How often do we actually consider the cost before we say yes? Instead, we think we can somehow be Superwoman, Super Teacher, and Supermom. We think we can do it all, but we can't. When we say *yes* to one thing, we are saying *no* to another. Too often those *no*'s are going to things that matter—our kids, our spouse, our health, our relationships, and even our spiritual life.

SOLUTION: Choose only the best things to say *yes* to. Then guard your time.

Instead of saying *yes* to everything, save your *yes* for the best things—the projects or responsibilities that can truly make a difference and to which you can give your full effort and energy.

Then, set boundaries to protect your time. Don't keep working until everything's done (there's *always* something more to do). Instead, determine ahead of time when you'll leave school for the day and how long you'll work at night. Block off time to simply be with your family or friends, and don't let yourself think about school during those times.

PROBLEM #7: You're staying stuck.

You know that one area of teaching that is driving you crazy? Maybe your students are always talking. Or you spend *forever* grading each night. Or a new policy that just came down the pipe is a *horrible* idea. Whatever it is—you feel stuck, trapped, helpless. But chances are there *is* something you can do—you've just gotta' put your thinking cap on.

THE SOLUTION: Think creatively.

Often there's a creative solution to our biggest frustrations if we ask the right questions. Instead of saying, "I can't do anything about this," start asking, "How could I make this work?"

Ask other teachers how they handle the situation. If you're struggling, invest in training. But, above all, pray about the situation. Ask God to give you clarity, and then ask yourself, "Is there an easier, better way to do this?"

Here's a quick example: I spoke with a teacher who was struggling with her school's requirement to administer at least 5-7 quizzes each grading period. She couldn't figure out how to fit them in, and she was getting frustrated. I suggested simply giving oral quizzes on the spot instead of typing them out ahead of time. "*Oh*," she said, "*I can do that?*"

"Of course!" I said. "Why not?"

And just like that the requirements were fulfilled with room left to breath.

PROBLEM #8: You're trying to be perfect.

Few things will drive you to despair faster than a pursuit of perfection. So please, stop getting frustrated with yourself that you're not yet the teacher you want to be. You must celebrate your progress, enjoy the journey, and remember that growth takes time.

THE SOLUTION: Celebrate progress and enjoy the journey.

You're not the teacher now that you will be in five years, but don't expect to get there overnight. Don't expect your students to be perfect overnight either.

Recognize perfectionism as the dangerous, unbiblical pursuit that it is. (It's often a direct result of our own pride — our own desire to be respected and to feel good about ourselves.) Then run from it. Cast it down. Enjoy the journey God is taking you on. Remember that you don't have everything under control but God sure does. And He never makes mistakes.

Journal/Discussion: What changes do you need to make to your habits and mindset?

Lesson 28:
Stress Busters

Not many people know stress like teachers do. There is always so much to do and no time to do it. Plus, we're literally responsible for dozens of lives all day long—and not just keeping them from bodily harm (which would be hard enough), but actually making sure they learn something, too. And not just something — but a lot of somethings. And not just the quadratic equation and the systems of the body, but good character as well.

Add to this already daunting task the challenges of unmotivated kids and disengaged parents (or, possibly worse, helicopter parents), the pressure of assessments, and the responsibility to care for your own family, and you've got the perfect recipe for a good old panic attack.

But while stress is common in the teaching profession, that doesn't mean that it *should* be—especially among Christian teachers. Consider this promise from Philippians 4:6-7: Be anxious for nothing, but in everything by prayer and supplication, with thanksgiving, let your requests be made known to God; and the peace of God, which surpasses all understanding, will guard your hearts and minds through Christ Jesus.

The promise is clear. So why do we have so much trouble experiencing it?

Perhaps we're worried about the future.

When we fret over days that lie ahead, we either haven't surrendered our future to God, or we do not trust Him to work it out. For example, we may be stressing about where we're going to teach next year because we secretly (or not so secretly) have our heart set on teaching at a certain school—as opposed to surrendering to teach wherever God places us. Or, we lose sleep over our students' test scores and our evaluations because we aren't trusting that God is in control of these things.

If we let all that go and surrender to what God has for us—if we trust Him that what He has is best—then we can stop being anxious or worried. Instead of looking out for our own desired outcome, we must surrender the results to God.

> *But seek first the kingdom of God and His righteousness,*
> *and all these things shall be added to you. Therefore do*
> *not worry about tomorrow, for tomorrow will worry*
> *about its own things. Sufficient for the day is its own trouble.*
> *—Matthew 6:33-34*

Remember, trust is a choice. If we are confident God's results are best, then we only need to do what we can. **We can blissfully leave the results entirely in His hands. To do that, we must first recognize the sources of our stress.**

So much of our anxiety comes from our worries about how we are perceived. We fret about how our administrations, parents, or fellow teachers perceive us. Too often, we take things personally and get upset when we feel we are not treated right. But honestly, does what they think matter? It only matters if it affects our testimony and how people perceive our God.

We can find freedom from people's perceptions by surrendering our ambitions to the Lord. On the days when we focus on pleasing God instead of people, everything runs more smoothly.

Have you surrendered your ego, your pride, to Him? Or do you hold your reputation as your hidden idol? Are you more concerned about your reputation than you are about loving others and serving God? When we're focused on what God thinks of our work, instead of what everyone else thinks, the anxiety falls away, and we're able to focus on what truly matters.

> *For am I now seeking the approval of man, or of God? Or am I trying to please man? If I were still trying to please man, I would not be a servant of Christ. —Galatians 1:10 (ESV)*

Often, anxiety comes when we're facing a situation that has us stumped. We're unsure, so we work ourselves into a frenzy trying to figure it out. Now on the one hand, God has given us creative minds to solve problems and find solutions. But we know we're going too far when the panic and anxiety start to crowd in—when we can't stop thinking about the problem.

We must surrender these questions to God and trust Him to guide us. Stop thinking with a one-track mind and give your concern to God, asking Him to bring clarity. That doesn't mean we stop talking to others or looking for answers. (God often uses those things to guide us.) However, we can choose to trust Him to guide us instead of leaning on our understanding.

> *Trust in the Lord with all your heart, And lean not on your*
> *own understanding; In all your ways acknowledge Him, And*
> *He shall direct your paths. —Proverbs 3:5-6*

Anxiety also comes when we don't want to deal with a particular challenge. We know our first-period class is going to be a trial, we dread that difficult parent coming in for a conference, or we're hoping against hope that Evan doesn't sling his ketchup-ridden fries at us—*again*. But in each case, we must trust God to guide the situation and surrender the outcome to Him. **We must change how we think about difficult situations.**

There is a reason He puts us in tough situations, and we must trust Him. His purpose for our trials will result in good. We often think we deserve an easy life, but that's simply not how God has called us to live. In fact, He's specifically called us to trials and suffering. **God could calm the waters, but then we'd never learn anything**. Instead, He uses challenges to teach us, grow us. And through the storms, we can be an unshakable, inextinguishable light for the Lord.

So in the worst of it, we can proclaim 2 Corinthians 12:10, *"Therefore I take pleasure in infirmities, in reproaches, in needs, in persecutions, in distresses, for Christ's sake. For when I am weak, then I am strong."*

We can find the purpose behind the pain as James admonishes. *"My brethren, count it all joy when you fall into various trials, knowing that the testing of your faith produces patience. But let patience have its perfect work, that you may be perfect and complete, lacking nothing". —James 1:2-4*

When we let go of our own expectations of ease, embrace God's plan (not ours) and choose to trust Him through it, we can finally teach without anxiety.

Journal/Discussion: Which of these stress-reducing mindset shifts resonated most with you? Why?

Lesson 29:
The Principal's Office

I can vividly remember the first time I was called into the principal's office, not as a student, but as a teacher. Okay, I'd probably been there a million times before for various reasons, but this was the first time the conversation was taking a less-than-ideal turn.

It was somewhere around October of my first year of teaching, and apparently I hadn't been doing the best job keeping my class in line. I knew I was struggling, but still, hearing it from the principal was no fun. Tears flooded toward my eyes. I barely held them back until I reached the safety of my car. Then the dam gave way.

Since then, I have had many conversations with administration—some that consisted of kudos and congratulations—and others that featured a critique of the amount of homework I gave, my grading methods, or how I'd handled a particular situation. But here's the thing about all the not-so-fun conversations: They produce the most growth.

We love to hear how great of a job we're doing or how wonderful our newest idea is. And that encouragement can be a huge morale booster. But it's actually the tough, constructive-criticism conversations that catapult us to the next level of excellence—if, that is, we accept them with the right attitude.

Too often we do the opposite. We decide our classroom is our domain, and we know what is best. We allow our feelings to get hurt, and we get defensive. Our heels dig in, and we refuse to move. And in doing so, we refuse to grow.

It's true that sometimes administrators implement bad policies or don't have all the facts, but we are way too quick to jump to that conclusion. Perhaps, more often than we even realize, they have insight and ideas that can make us better—even if the plan sounds horrible at first.

Next time you face constructive criticism, here's a few things to keep in mind:

When Facing Constructive Criticism ...

1. Be humble.

Nothing will stop our growth faster than our own pride. Yes, it hurts to hear we may need to change something or that we're falling short in some area or another. But as defensive as we feel, we need to instead be humble. We must stop and listen to what our administrator is saying and be open to new ideas. We must realize that no matter how long we've been teaching, no matter how many students and parents say, "Yeah. She's a great teacher!" we can always be better.

2. Realize there may be a better way.

Often when I've had these conversations with administration, it's not that my way was necessarily wrong—but there was a *better* way. When I stopped trying to defend my way and started listening and looking for the *better* way, I was actually thankful. They still weren't the most fun conversations, but my classroom was better because of them.

3. **Have an open-minded dialogue.**

We all know that administrators are not infallible. Sometimes their ideas aren't the best, and sometimes they don't understand what's going on in your classroom. But once again—the answer is not to get defensive and shut out their suggestions. Instead, have an open-minded dialogue. Explain your point of view, but be genuinely open to new ideas and a new plan you can develop together.

4. **Be excited about the growth process.**

You want to grow and be a better teacher. (I know because you're still reading this book). But you need to embrace the fact that growth is often a bit painful. It's tough to change lesson plans, teaching styles, or discipline methods. And it's no fun to get a less-than-favorable evaluation or to hear all the ways you need to improve. But the sooner we embrace the growth process, the happier we will be and the faster we will grow.

So the next time constructive criticism comes along, recognize it for the growth opportunity that it is, do exactly the opposite of what you feel like doing, and embrace it wholeheartedly.

Journal/Discussion: How do you typically handle constructive criticism? What piece of constructive criticism has most helped you grow?

Lesson 30:
Attack of the Sauls

Have you ever felt like an administrator was out to get you? Like they were devising your demise? Well, that's what David faced. He showed loyalty, dedication, and passion, but a jealous administrator started scheming against him. Saul undermined David whenever he could, made horrible decisions, handed him the worst assignments, and plotted against him.

What did David do? Surprisingly, he didn't call up his union. He didn't go on a crusade to defend his rights. In fact, when an opportunity arose for David to stab his administrator in the back, he refused. He did something radically different. And maybe we should, too.

Here are some unconventional—but Biblical—ways to deal with a difficult administrator.

1. **Take your burdens to God and leave them.**

   We bring our troubles to Him. We hit our knees. But too often we stand back up with our load in tow. When we do that, we're missing the point. God wants us to give Him our concerns and drop them.

   Leave them. That means we decide to trust Him with everything involving our administrator—what decisions they make, how we implement those decisions, and what they think of us—everything.

Stop right now. Give your concerns to God in prayer. Place Him in charge of the situation and follow His lead.

Casting all your care upon Him, for He cares for you. –I Peter 5:7

2. Stop worrying about what your administrator thinks of you.

We all want to be respected. We want our administrators to think highly of us as professionals, but worrying about what they think is stressful. Worse, it's harmful. It keeps us from the truth: we are called to work for God, not man. We must realize that when we fret about how our front-office leaders perceive us, pride is rearing its ugly head—trying its best to make sure we look good.

Your administrator may have a lot of power. You may be concerned about a raise or your evaluation. You may wonder whether or not you'll be re-hired for the next school year. But remember, God is the one who is ultimately in control. Whatever happens to you because of your administrator is part of His plan. You can trust Him; you can count on His promises. When you stop worrying about your administrator's perceptions of you, you'll feel the burdens roll off your back.

And whatever you do, do it heartily, as to the Lord and not to men, knowing that from the Lord you will receive the reward of the inheritance; for you serve the Lord Christ.
–Colossians 3:23-24

Do I seek to please men? For if I still pleased men, I would not be a bondservant of Christ. –Galatians 1:10

3. **Let go of what you think you deserve.**

    The world tells us we're supposed to be treated well. That life
    should be cordial and carefree. The Bible paints a different
    picture. God says our lives are meant for His glory, not our
    pleasure. He never promised an easy life, but He guarantees
    He'll be our strength, our guide, our rock, and our rest. The
    Lord assures us that everything He allows serves a purpose in
    our lives. He will work all of it together for good if we let Him.

    Many times, we focus on how unfair our situation is. We complain
    rather than leaning into God and learning the lessons He wants
    to show us through our trials. A critical, micromanaging, or
    unreasonable boss can be used by God to refine our character,
    teach us His truths, and bring us closer to Him. He can only do
    this when we surrender the matter to His care.

    And we know that all things work together for good to those who
    love God, to those who are the called according to His purpose.
    For whom He foreknew, He also predestined to be conformed to
    the image of His Son, that He might be the firstborn among many
    brethren. –Romans 8:28-29

4. **Choose to give grace and the benefit of the doubt.**

    We tend to jump to conclusions about our administrator's
    decisions. We're sure they made the wrong choice. We believe
    they acted inappropriately. Maybe they have. But is it possible
    we don't know all the facts?

    You know how tough a school day can be. You unintentionally
    snap at the poor student who asks the same question you
    just answered eighteen times. Well, sometimes our leaders
    experience similar moments. It doesn't excuse their behavior,
    but we can extend grace. We can choose empathy. Think of the

difficulties of their job. Understand they're probably dealing with tough situations—with things we know nothing about.

The same holds true for policy decisions. Sometimes administrators enact bad strategies. Again, there may be considerations of which we are unaware. The policy seems misguided from our perspective, but maybe we don't have all the facts.

Bottom line: the more we choose to give grace and the benefit of the doubt, the more we release ourselves from the chains of judgment. And that, my dear teacher, is good for everyone.

Therefore, as the elect of God, holy and beloved, put on tender mercies, kindness, humility, meekness, longsuffering; bearing with one another, and forgiving one another, if anyone has a complaint against another; even as Christ forgave you, so you also must do. But above all these things put on love, which is the bond of perfection. And let the peace of God rule in your hearts, to which also you were called in one body; and be thankful. –Colossians 3:12-15

5. **Look for creative ways to deal with challenging demands**.

   When an administrator gives us a difficult or unreasonable requirement, we have a choice. Get frustrated and grumble. Or, generate a creative solution and make it work. Try asking yourself, "How can I meet this requirement in a way that fits in my current system, doesn't take too much time, and benefits the students?" You might not think there's a solution out there, but chances are, one exists.

   Let me give an example.

   When I taught math, I used to take off points for students who didn't show their work, or who didn't use graph paper for graphing. One day my administrator called me into his office.

"I'm sorry, I'm going to have to ask you to stop taking off points for these things," he said. "It's against school policy."

Now my administrator was terrific, which helped my attitude. But I was still frustrated and worried. If I didn't take off points, my students' work would digress. Wouldn't it?

Then I thought about it. What could I do instead that would meet this requirement from my administration but also solve the problem for my classroom? I decided to give my students their full credit. But then I would require them to redo the homework the correct way. Presto. Problem solved. My new system ended up working better than my original plan.

That's just one example. The point is, there is often a way to make things work if you're willing to look for a creative solution. Pray for guidance. Talk to other teachers. Ask how they do it. Ask yourself: How can I make this work? Keep at it until you find your answer.

6. **Focus on doing the best job you can for your students.**

   When work has you in a tizzy, take a breath and remember you're here for your students. Think about them. Do your best for them. Focus on all the things you *can* control to help them learn and grow.

7. **Find others who will support you.**

   If your administrator isn't giving you the help you need, find someone else who will. It may be another teacher or administrator at your school. It may be a friend from church or someone you meet online. Our Facebook group provides a place to encourage each other. Go to **www.teach4theheart.com/group** to request to join.

8. Think win-win.

When you talk with your administration, always approach it with a mutual gain in mind. Start from the realization that they have the same goals. Remember you are on the same team, even when it doesn't feel like it.

Don't view the situation as a competition—you versus them. That doesn't help anything. Instead, keep in mind everyone wants what is best for the students. You may disagree about how to get there. But start your conversations with the right attitude. Don't be afraid to say something like, "We both want what's best for the students, but I'm having trouble understanding this policy. Do you mind explaining why?"

Chances are, they will share their reasoning.

9. Seek first to understand, then to be understood.

We can go into a meeting and spout off our pent-up thoughts, but that may or may not go over so well. Instead, start your conversation by trying to understand your administrator's point of view. Ask questions. Genuinely listen to their responses. You'll often discover there's been a misunderstanding.

Either way, you'll gain valuable insight that will allow you to present your viewpoint in a way that is relevant to them. When you seek first to understand, then to be understood, you'll be amazed at how differently the conversation flows. You'll find out progress is possible.

10. Continue to pray and trust God.

No matter what happens, determine to pray for your administrator—and not that they will get fired. Pray God will work in their lives and give them wisdom. As you come to the Lord, surrender to His plan and trust Him. We may not understand why He allows certain scenarios to unfold.

We can rest in His arms, knowing He is indeed in control. He loves us. He will use even the hardest times for His purposes. We must remember Paul's words to the Philippians: "Be anxious for nothing, but in everything by prayer and supplication, with thanksgiving, let your requests be made known to God; and the peace of God, which surpasses all understanding, will guard your hearts and minds through Christ Jesus" (Philippians 4:6-7).

That's what David did. He determined to trust God and leave the situation in His control. When given the opportunity to ruin his horrible administrator, he did nothing. He refused to take into his own hands what belonged only in God's.

Do you remember how it all turned out for David? He became one of the most famous kings in history. God was using all those difficulties to prepare him to rule His people well.

So when you're frustrated, discouraged, and ready to call it quits, remember God works in mysterious ways. Surrender to what He wants to do in your life. Most likely, you won't be a king. But you never know what He is preparing you for.

Journal/Discussion: How did you typically handle disagreement with administration? What do you want to do differently in the future?

Lesson 31:
The Complaint Department is Closed

"The complaint department is closed."

This phrase was often repeated (and occasionally mocked) during the annual summer missions program our youth department conducted when I was growing up. It even showed up as a comic each year in the training booklet. Why? Well, because the week of our missions program was always crazy busy, and we had tons of work to do. Our youth workers didn't want us to waste everyone's time and energy by complaining.

Sound familiar?

We could all fantasize for a moment about our school posting a sign on the door reading, "The complaint department is closed"— not just to students but to parents too. If all the grumbling ended, we'd save a ton of time and energy. We'd be free to focus on teaching. Stress levels would plummet. It would be glorious!

Or would it?

If all parents' complaints were just that—complaining—then we should close up the complaint department and call it a day. But more often than we care to admit, they're actually not complaints. They're concerns. Real concerns about real challenges their child is facing in your classroom.

Yes, it hurts. You've poured your heart into your students, into your classroom. You've worked hard. You've done everything you can. Meanwhile parents are going behind your back, undermining you to your administrators. You're frustrated, discouraged, feeling a little betrayed, and maybe even worried about the future of your job.

But you have a choice to make: get upset, blame the parents, stress about what your administrator thinks about you, and allow the complaints to stink up your whole life like a three-month-old lunch stuffed in the bottom of a locker. Or, choose to look at the complaint as an opportunity to grow as a teacher. Use it to address the parents' core concerns and improve your communication and relationship with the family.

To grow through complaints, we must realize the complaint could stem from three different sources:

1. **There may be a misunderstanding between you and the parent.**

2. **There may be something that you as the teacher could have handled better or could fix going forward.**

3. **The parent may have unreasonable expectations.**

Now we love to jump right to that final conclusion and declare the parent unreasonable. They simply don't like us, and they're out to get us fired. But more often than not there are other factors in play. Maybe the parent is acting unreasonably because they don't understand something. Or maybe, even though the parent is being difficult, there's still something we can change that will make the situation better for everyone.

Remember how frustrated I was about having to change my homework grading policy? What I didn't share was how the whole situation started with a parent complaint. While I felt the requirement was unreasonable, there was, in fact, a better way I could handle the matter. The new solution I created turned out to be better than my original policy.

The point is that just because you think a parent is being difficult doesn't mean you shouldn't *also* try to clear up misunderstandings and look for opportunities to improve. Which brings us to our first step in handling parents' complaints.

1. **Choose to look at the complaint as an opportunity for growth.**

   When you first hear about the complaint, you're going to feel betrayed, hurt, frustrated, and probably more than a little defensive. But take a deep breath. Pray. Realize you have the power to change how you view this situation. You can choose to be upset and defensive, or you can choose to use this as an opportunity to learn and grow. If you let them, most parent complaints can push you to become even better. Or they may provide deeper insight into your student's home lives or how they learn.

The key is to take what appears, at first, to be the beginning of a terrible, horrible, no good, very bad day and reframe it as an opportunity for growth, recognizing God is working even in circumstances like this, to teach us something and to make us more like Him.

And we know that all things work together for good to those who love God, to those who are the called according to His purpose. For whom He foreknew, He also predestined to be conformed to the image of His Son, that He might be the firstborn among many brethren. –Romans 8:28-29

2. **Seek to genuinely understand not just the complaint but also the underlying concerns.**

    When the complaint is first brought up, you're going to want to push back. You'll want to explain all the reasons why you did what you did or why you have the policy you have. If you can stop yourself, please do. You'll have time to explain, but that shouldn't be your immediate goal. First, you need to understand what the parent is thinking. And I don't mean a surface understanding of "they think I give too much homework." No, you need to genuinely try to understand not only their point of view but also what's causing their complaint.

    The complaint itself is often superficial. There is almost always some kind of underlying fear or concern that lies underneath the initial gripe. For example: take a parent who's complaining about the amount of homework you're giving. They may actually be concerned about their son's exhaustion, due to his not starting his homework until after basketball practice and not getting to bed until 11:00. Or they may not truly be concerned about the **amount** of homework at all but are actually frustrated because their son is failing math. They might not know how to help him with his homework, and they spend two torturous hours a night agonizing over it to no avail.

These concerns are what you *really* want to address, and it will take some good listening and maybe some well-placed questions to get to them. But once you understand exactly how they see the situation and what their core concerns actually are, then you can much more easily clear up any misunderstandings and address the real issues.

3. **Reflect honestly on the situation and get outside feedback if needed.**

    If you can't immediately clear up the problem by explaining an obvious misunderstanding, take an honest look at your practices and policies. Ask yourself what you could do to address this complaint and its underlying concerns. This doesn't necessarily mean you've done anything wrong in the past. But there might be a **better** way of doing things in the future.

    Don't let yourself off the hook if you think the parent is being unreasonable. They may be, but there could still be something you could change that would improve the learning experience for everyone. Spend time thinking about their underlying concern, and ask yourself how you can address **the real issue.**

    If you're coming up blank (or can't get past your frustration with the parent), get feedback from someone you trust to tell you the truth. This is *not* the time to run to the person who always tells you what you want to hear. Instead, seek counsel from a trusted friend, fellow teacher, or administrator and ask them if they can think of anything you could do differently. Honestly consider any suggestions they give you.

4. **Discuss your conclusions with your administrator.**

If the parents have complained to your administration, you'll want to keep them in the loop with any realizations you come to. Your administrator will be happy to hear about any new policies you're implementing, as they're likely concerned about both your reaction to the complaint and the parents' concerns in the matter.

If after careful consideration and discussion, it's clear the parent truly is being unreasonable and there's nothing you can or should change, discuss this with your administrator, too. Stay teachable and ask them if they have any suggestions— either a change that you hadn't thought of or advice for interacting with the parent going forward.

5. **Meet again with the parent to discuss next steps.**

If the parent has gone over your head to complain, the relationship is somewhat broken. And as frustrated as you are, you must do what you can to repair it. Meet with them and have an open, honest conversation about what you're doing differently and also what you're *not*. Explain why you *didn't* make certain changes, but don't get defensive. Instead, take the approach that you both want what is best for their student, and have the hard conversations about what that looks like.

Remember back to the beginning when you were listening for the underlying concerns beneath the parent's initial complaint?

Make sure **that** is what you're addressing. Even if the parent is not thrilled with your answer to their complaint, they should be able to see that you care about their underlying concerns and are looking for ways to address them.

6. **Let it go.**

Sometimes you make all the changes you can, do your best to say all the right things, and the parent still walks away upset. At this point, you've got to let it go. Seek to continue improving. Commit to keep on loving the student and not to hold this conflict against the parents. And simply choose to move on. You have to, or it will eat you alive.

If you're struggling, take your burden to Jesus and give it to Him. Bring your hurt, your frustration, your confusion, and leave it at His feet. Don't you dare stand up from praying and pick your burden back up again. Give it to Him, leave it there, and every time you start to worry about it again, take it right back to His feet.

If you take this approach when parents complain, staying humble and addressing parents' core concerns, you might be amazed at the strong relationships that emerge. Not to mention the wealth of insights you come away with and the new, creative solutions you discover.

And who knows. You may even find it in your heart to be thankful the complaint department wasn't closed.

Journal/Discussion: What is your typical reaction when a parent complains? What do you want to do differently going forward?

Lesson 32:
Growth Takes Time

Have you ever felt like you're not making any progress? You're pouring your heart out for your students, and they're not getting it. It seems like everything you say is going in one ear and out the other.

Or maybe your personal growth or career as a teacher feels stagnant. You're struggling more than you thought you would and you can't seem to reach the next level.

We've all been there. But when we start to get frustrated with our apparent lack of progress, we have to remember one crucial principle: growth takes time. It doesn't happen overnight. It happens step by step, little by little. Moment by moment. Day by day.

I sure wish our desire to be a better teacher, spouse, parent, and friend meant we would wake up the next morning having mastered all of these roles. I wish our desire to know God more meant our relationship with Him would grow by leaps and bounds by the end of the week. But that's not how it works.

Reflect—look back ten years and see how much God has grown you. It's been gradual, bit by bit. You've learned, grown, matured, mastered new skills, and deepened your understanding of Him.

But while there have been some exciting ah-ha moments, most of the growth happened slowly.

So when we start to get frustrated, to feel like we're never going to figure out how to manage a classroom, never going to know what to say when our students ask us a hard question, never going to have victory over a particular personal struggle—we need to remember that growth takes time. **We need to look back and see how far we've come and look forward with anticipation to the growth we're going to see over time. In a word, we need to be *patient*.**

We must also remember this principle when we feel like we aren't making any progress with a particular student (or maybe with all of them). When it seems like nothing is happening, when you've been working with them for months and they still don't get it, when you're about to throw your hands up in frustration, don't give up. Remember that growth takes time not only in us but in our students, too.

This is particularly hard for new teachers. I remember thinking as a first-year teacher that I hadn't seen any turnarounds, and I was a little disappointed that I didn't have any transformation stories like all my fellow teachers did. But then something incredible happened over the next couple years. I saw those students whom I'd poured my time, love, and focus into start to grow up, start to mature, start to make some real progress. And it was incredibly rewarding.

I remember one student in particular who simply didn't like me and was pretty much trying to make my life miserable. Over time, she made a complete 180 and turned into one of my biggest blessings. But here's the key—this change did not happen overnight. In fact, it did not even happen over the course of a few weeks or even months. It wasn't until our third year together that she came to me and said, "Wow, I can't believe I did all those stupid things as a 6th grader." Talk about an incredible moment! But it took a long time to get there. And the change happened— you guessed it—little by little.

So yes, there will be moments of epiphany, moments of breakthrough, days that you think, "Wow, we just made great progress!" But there are so many more days where it seems like nothing is happening, nothing is moving, and you're not even sure you're going in the right direction. During these times, remember that growth is happening, even when you can't notice. That is, as long as you're open to it.

Journal/Discussion: Can you look back and see growth that at the time didn't seem to be happening? What frustrations have you experienced when you wanted to see progress more quickly than you were?

Lesson 33:
Prayer Changes YOU

We've all heard the saying *prayer changes things*, and of course, it does. But more significantly, prayer changes us. It re-orients our hearts and opens them to hear God's truths.

Throughout this section, I've encouraged you to take your challenges, frustrations, and concerns to God in prayer. I've stressed the importance of leaving them there and choosing to trust God's plan even when we don't understand it.

Now it's time to put that into action. Take a few moments to pray about the challenges you're facing right now, about the things that stress and concern you. Give them to God, choose to desire His will above your own, and determine to leave them with Him when you say *Amen*.

Journal/Put it into Practice: Spend time in prayer right now about the difficulties you are currently facing. You may also want to pray for the following:

- That you would depend on His Spirit and not on your own strength.

- That God would give you a love for each of your students, especially the ones who try your patience.

- That God would enable you to give grace and the benefit of the doubt.

- That you would trust Him in all things and remember He is in control.

- That your administration would have wisdom to make the right decisions.

Resources

Check out these resources for more help staying encouraged:

FREE Training: Teach without Anxiety

If you find yourself often worried or stressed, join us in this free training where we explore in more detail how you can trust God and teach without anxiety.

Join for free at **www.teach4theheart.com/anxietytraining**.

Teach Uplifted Program

Do you find yourself continually frustrated? Full of worry or anxiety? Join us in this 6-week program to renew your passion for teaching by finding joy and peace in Christ.

Find out more at **www.teachuplifted.com**.

Or, get the devotional book at **www.teach4theheart.com/devotions**.

Part 4:
Take Heart and Make
a Bigger Difference

*Let your light so shine before men, that they may see your good works
and glorify your Father in heaven.* –Matthew 5:16

Armed with a strong classroom management plan, balanced by
wise time-management, and centered through deep trust in and
joy from Christ, you're now equipped to make a bigger difference
than ever in your students' hearts and lives.

Don't focus on the challenges, the restrictions, the indifference.
Take heart and look to Christ, determined to follow the Spirit's
leading each day and shine His light in your classroom

Make a bigger difference.

Lesson 34:
Why We Teach

Do you ever stop and ask yourself why you're a teacher? And I'm not talking about the times of exasperation when we throw up our hands and wonder what on earth we're doing here.

Have you truly answered the question of why you teach? Maybe you're passionate about your subject. Maybe you love interacting with students, or maybe you live for those the "Ah-ha" moments when a concept finally clicks. But if those are the only reason you're a teacher, you're missing some key components. As Christian teachers, our mission must go beyond passing on knowledge or even inspiring a love of learning. We should be looking for God to change lives in our classrooms.

No matter where you teach, this mission must be foremost in your mind. You must never forget that God's Word is true and that He is the answer to all of life's problems, even if others don't believe in Him or don't want to hear about it.

If you teach in a public school, you are limited by laws, policies, and expectations. But don't believe for a second that God is bound by the laws that declare He isn't welcome. He still does powerful works, so be looking for Him to work through you.

Of course, you cannot stand up in class and declare "thus says the Lord," **but you should be keenly aware that He *is* the answer.** Pray that He will work in your students' lives and ask Him to show you what you should say and do. Be a bright light pushing back darkness as described in Matthew 5:15-16: *"Nor do they light a lamp and put it under a basket, but on a lampstand, and it gives light to all who are in the house. Let your light so shine before men, that they may see your good works and glorify your Father in heaven."*

If you teach in a Christian school, your mission is to help your students become committed followers of Jesus Christ, and (hopefully) there's nothing holding you back. So be bold. Speak truth every chance you get, and be intentional about leading kids to Christ; discipling them day in and day out.

Make disciples who will make more disciples. Keep this in the forefront of your mind, and always look for opportunities to draw students' hearts to Christ.

And the things that you have heard from me among many witnesses, commit these to faithful men who will be able to teach others also. —2 Timothy 2:2

Journal/Discussion: What is your ultimate mission as a Christian teacher? How can you keep this in the forefront of your mind?

Lesson 35:
Love Conquers All

Love is powerful. In our homes and in our classroom, love is
what makes the most impact, what changes hearts and minds.
We've seen its power, yet we struggle at times to demonstrate true,
genuine love, especially when a particular kiddo is not acting
lovable. But since love *is* such a powerful force, maybe loving is
what we should focus on when things are going wrong—when
Bradley's temper is out of control or when Nicole seems to be
ignoring everything we say.

I Corinthians 13:13 states, "And now abide faith, hope, love, these
three; but the greatest of these is love."

Love is not a feeling. Love is a choice. On the days when love is
hardest, we must choose to show love. And when we're wondering
how on earth to do that, I Corinthians 13 lights the way.

Loving Like God Loves

1. **Love is patient and kind.**

   Oh, this is easy to say but hard to live out. When Maya blurts
   out an answer for the 457th time today, I'm not always patient.
   And how many times have we teachers reacted to the question
   "What are we supposed to do again?" with something less than

kindness? We know we love our kids, but are we showing it to them by being patient and kind?

2. **Love does not seek its own.**

As teachers, we know what it means to put others first. We live to serve our students, but that doesn't mean selfishness can't slip in. When ungraded papers start to swallow our desks, we can become more task-focused than student-focused. But genuine love doesn't seek out what's best for us—it gives and gives and gives some more.

3. **Love is not easily provoked.**

Your students know how to push all the right buttons, don't they? We've all had moments where we wanted to scream at someone. Hopefully you've never actually hurled chalk at a student, but we've all responded with less than complete control on occasion. True, genuine love, though, is not easily provoked. It loves even in the most frustrating moments.

4. **Love thinks no evil.**

Think about that student who seems impossible to handle. You know, the one who you secretly wish would transfer to another school. That student is actually the one who needs your love the most. They're the one who desperately needs someone in their corner—rooting them on. Believe it or not, that kid could turn out to be your biggest blessing if you love patiently and consistently.

5. **Love does not rejoice in iniquity but rejoices in the truth.**

Our society believes that if you disagree with how someone is behaving, that's hate. The Bible says otherwise. If you truly love someone, you won't allow them to continue down a destructive path. Genuine love speaks the truth, humbly pointing out wrong and showing the right way. Correcting and guiding students is an outpouring of love, as long as it's just that—done in love.

6. Love never fails.

On the days when everything is going wrong and Wesley's snide comment feels like the last straw, love doesn't fail. When grades are due by 5:00 and you have to stop and break up a fight, love doesn't fail. It endures all things. It bears all things. Love always loves.

By now you probably think there's only one word to describe this type of love: *impossible*. You're right. We produce this love in ourselves this way because it's not a human love. It's a Divine love. It's God's love.

Love is listed as the first fruit of the Spirit in Galatians 5:22. That means love is the result of the Spirit's work in our lives, and the only way we can love like this is if He is loving through us. To truly love, we need more of the Spirit in our lives. We must deepen our relationship with God through prayer, and we must yield our lives to the Spirit and allow Him to work through us.

This won't be an overnight change. It's a daily—no, moment-by-moment—decision. Will we spend time with Him? Will we yield to Him in the most difficult moments? Will we allow Him to change us one little step at a time?

Lord, please change me today.

Journal/Discussion: When do you find it most difficult to love your students? How has Christ helped you to demonstrate His love?

Lesson 36:
Apples Come from Apple Trees

But the fruit of the Spirit is love, joy, peace, longsuffering (patience), kindness, goodness, faithfulness, gentleness, self-control. Against such there is no law. —Galatians 5:22-23

Imagine the power of your testimony—how attractive the Gospel would appear to your students, parents, and colleagues—if your actions were always full of love, if your heart was overflowing with joy, and if you had peace amidst the chaos. Imagine the difference you would evidence if you consistently demonstrated patience, were kind and good, evidenced strong faith, had the humility of meekness, and consistently practiced self-control.

But this is not pie-in-the-sky idealism. This is the life Christ wants for us, the fruit (or result) of the Spirit in our lives. These are essential traits of the Christian life, qualities we could use an extra dose of in our teaching. The problem comes when we view the fruit of the spirit from one of these false standpoints:

1. **A Christian to-do list**

   If we spend our best effort working on our self-control, endeavoring to be kind, or searching for peace, we are missing the point. These character traits are fruits (results) of the Spirit. Trying to instill these traits into our lives on our own is like trying to grow apples without an apple tree. It simply cannot be done. The fruit of the Spirit must be grown by the Holy Spirit in our lives. He is the one who does the work in us and produces His fruit.

That's why our relationship with God is so vital. If we want Him to produce His fruit in our lives, we must have more of the Spirit in our lives. We must spend time with Him in prayer and seek Him through His Word.

2. An unattainable ideal

Sometimes we focus our energy as Christians in the wrong places. Well, not wrong, but less important places. We try to be a light in the world by coming up with clever ways to get people into church. Or we focus our energy on the outside—trying to look like "good Christians" so others will see a difference.

Why do we do that? Maybe we don't think it's possible to actually evidence the fruit of the spirit. I've heard wonderful Christians say, "The Bible says we're supposed to show the world we're Christians by our love, but we're not doing so well with that, so we need to show them in these other ways."

No. God's way is the best way. He wants to do His work in our hearts. Furthermore, He is ready and able to change us, if we yield ourselves to Him and allow Him to do His work. The fruit of the Spirit is the difference God wants to see in us—the way He has designed for us to make the Gospel attractive to a lost world (and floundering teens). These are the traits He values, so are we focusing on them? Are we asking the Spirit to develop them in us?

Do we believe that He can? Are we valuing them and honoring them when we see them in others? Do we desire to grow in these areas in our own lives?

God wants to produce His fruit in our hearts, to not only transform our personal life but also make us radical examples in our schools and classrooms. So let's not view them as a 'to-do' list that we can somehow work hard enough to attain—nor as an unattainable ideal we could never live up to.

Instead, let's seek God's will. Let's honor these traits, deeply desire this fruit, and yield to the Spirit. As we grow closer to Him each day and choose to yield our hearts to Him, He will work in us to develop love, joy, and peace. He will help us be more patient, kind, good, and meek, and to develop self-control.

Journal/Discussion: How do *you* view the fruit of the Spirit? Are you asking God to produce His fruit in you?

Lesson 37:
Facts and Opinions

What do you think of these definitions?

A **fact** is a statement that can be proven true or false. An **opinion** is a statement that expresses a belief, value, or feeling and cannot be proved true or false.

They're familiar definitions that are being taught across the country. But are they true?

Absolutely not.

Although popular opinion would have us affirm that beliefs are subjective, and that value statements cannot inherently be true or false but are a matter of personal opinion, we must never let these wrong philosophies invade our thinking. We must remember that God's Word is absolute truth, regardless of whether anyone else agrees. Biblical beliefs and values are not merely opinions. They are absolute truth, based on the inspired Word of the Divine Creator.

Ask your unbelieving colleagues, and they may say you are foolish for trusting an ancient book and an unseen God. They may argue that each opinion is equally valid as long as it is sincere, or that you can't possibly know that your beliefs are more true than anyone else's.

But this is the world's wisdom. As Christians, we must ask ourselves, are we going to trust God or the world?

> *Let no one deceive himself. If anyone among you seems to be wise in this age, let him become a fool that he may become wise. For the wisdom of this world is foolishness with God. For it is written, "He catches the wise in their own craftiness"; and again, "The Lord knows the thoughts of the wise, that they are futile." —I Corinthians 3:18-20*
>
> *Beware lest anyone cheat you through philosophy and empty deceit, according to the tradition of men, according to the basic principles of the world, and not according to Christ.* —Colossians 2:8

No matter what situation comes up in your classroom—from girl drama to college advice to a student who comes out to you—if you want to lead students in the right direction, you must start with a Biblical view of the situation. And that starts by recognizing that **what God has designed is best for everyone.**

God knows everything and is perfectly good. He designed this world, designed us. If anyone knows the best way to live life, the best way to function as a society, don't you think it's God? Why on earth do we think that we're somehow smarter than Him, that we've somehow evolved past His moral law?

God didn't give us His commands for the fun of it. He gave them because they are the best way to live, because they are the foundation of a stable and healthy society, and to show us our need for Him. God loves us desperately and wants what is best for us. He knows His commands are the path of life and blessing, so He asks us to follow them. He knows when we reject them or deviate from them, we set ourselves on a dangerous path that leads to sorrow and destruction, so He warns us strongly against the dangers.

> *You are good, and do good; Teach me Your statutes. You,*
> *through Your commandments, make me wiser than my*
> *enemies; For they are ever with me. Through Your precepts I get*
> *understanding; Therefore I hate every false way. The entirety of*
> *Your word is truth, And every one of Your righteous judgments*
> *endures forever. –Psalm 119: 68, 98, 104, 160*

We cannot and should not expect everyone to believe what we believe or act the way we act, but where we have opportunities, we should always champion the Biblical way because it's the best way. We should always champion the truth because it's the truth.

If you teach in a public school, you cannot tell people, "The Bible says to be content with what you have," but you can talk about the virtue of contentment and why it matters. And when it comes to controversial issues—issues where our culture and the Bible stand vastly apart—remember that God loves us, that He knows what He's talking about, and that His ways truly are best for everyone—whether they know Him personally or not.

As teachers, we can and should be concerned about the culture we are shaping for the next generation. Will we go along with what's expected, encouraging young people towards all kinds of behavior that is bad for them, bad for their families, and bad for our society in general? Or will we do what we can to encourage young people towards the paths that are truly best for them?

As we consider these questions, we often fall prey to a huge misconception—the concept of a sacred/secular split. It goes something like this: the sacred (i.e. faith) is private while the secular is public.

In other words, many Christians essentially divide their lives and work into two parts. In one part is their faith. It's genuine. They love God, they read their Bible, maybe even teach Sunday school or lead a Bible club. But their faith is for their private life—for their soul. It has little if anything to do with secular issues. Thus, they go to church and worship on Sunday, but when speaking with a student on Monday, they don't see how their faith has anything to do with that. Or, even if they do think the Bible has something to offer, they don't see it as their place to bring that view into the secular sphere.

But the Biblical view is exactly what the secular sphere needs. Remember that God's truths are best for everyone. That means there *is* no split between the sacred and secular. We might create one in our minds, but it doesn't actually exist. We are thinking incorrectly. God has created truths that are universal, that will help those who adhere to them, regardless of whether they are saved or not. His truths plow through all barriers and belong in the public sphere just as much as in the private sphere.

As teachers, our job is to teach the truth and to create the best learning environment possible for our students. But if in the process of trying to teach the truth, we reject the Bible and lean on the world's philosophies instead, we are actually lying to our students and aren't doing a good job at all.

If you're thinking, "But I'm not allowed to bring up God or the Bible," you're missing the best part—these truths are universal. That means they can be taught apart from the Bible, that you can defend His truths from a logical or scientific standpoint without mentioning God once.

Ask yourself if you've started to compartmentalize your faith in this way. Do you value your faith on a personal level but bristle at the thought of applying Biblical truth to "secular" issues? Do you embrace a "separate of church and state" viewpoint, thinking that your views can and should be set aside when you step in the classroom? If so, it's time to reject this sacred/secular split and embrace the joyous reality that God's truths are meant for our whole lives and our whole society.

(For further discussion on this topic, I strongly recommend Nancy Pearcey's book *Total Truth*.)

> *You are the salt of the earth; but if the salt loses its flavor, how shall it be seasoned? It is then good for nothing but to be thrown out and trampled underfoot by men. You are the light of the world. A city that is set on a hill cannot be hidden. Nor do they light a lamp and put it under a basket, but on a lampstand, and it gives light to all who are in the house. Let your light so shine before men, that they may see your good works and glorify your Father in heaven. —Matthew 5:13-16*

Journal/Discussion: Have you fallen prey to the sacred / secular split? How do you need to reframe your thinking?

Lesson 38:
Creation, the Fall, and Redemption

We've laid the groundwork for bringing Biblical truth into everything you do (including your public life in the classroom), but first we need to understand how God views the issue you're encountering.

The Bible is the supreme source of truth, and in many cases, it is crystal clear. Other times, however, the Bible doesn't speak directly to an issue, and we must apply Biblical truth and a Biblical view of our world to understand the truth. In these cases, it's extremely beneficial to view an issue through the lens of the three key aspects of Biblical history: creation, the fall, and redemption

For example, let's take this framework and examine a common modern-day question: what is a family? (Or, perhaps more accurately, what *should* a family look like?)

Creation: We must always start with the fact that God created us and designed us. As such, He knows what's best. In regards to the question of the family, take God's original design. He created a husband and wife and put them together. He designed marriage and intended it to last a lifetime. He purposed that children be born to married parents and that families should be strong and devoted. This was His original pattern, and it was good.

The Fall: Next, we must consider how the fall—or sin and its curse—has affected God's original plan. In the case of the family, the fall has brought a multitude of problems and deviations. Sins of the heart such as pride and selfishness cause problems within marriage and often lead to divorce.

Satan has brought confusion to the minds of many and has led them to seek affection and marriage in someone of the same gender, something that was not part of God's original plan. Children are born outside of marriage because couples do not wish to follow God's pattern. Parents are often selfish and don't put enough energy and love into raising their children. All of these deviations cause grievous heartache for all involved, and children often struggle because of it.

We must remember that deviations from God's plan always lead to pain and heartache.

Redemption: Through Jesus, God has made a way to heal what is broken and to restore us to His original design.

In regards to the family: Christ has the power to heal all the brokenness—to restore marriages, build strong families, break the power of same-sex attraction, and empower parents to raise wise children. This is the ultimate hope for our society at large and for individuals in particular. For those who are not saved, still, the closer they can follow God's plan, the better things will go and, ultimately, the happier they and their family will be. The more families that follow God's model, the more stable and productive our society will be.

This is just one example. Try using this three-part framework the next time a question or issue comes up and see if it helps you reframe the topic from a Biblical perspective.

Journal/Discussion: Think of another difficult question or issue you face in your classroom or personal life. Practice applying the three-part framework of Creation, the Fall, and Redemption to this issue. If you need help, join the discussion in our book club at **www.teach4theheart.com/bookclub.**

Lesson 39:
Walking with God

Seek the LORD and His strength; Seek His face evermore!
–I Corinthians 16:11

Prayer and our relationship with God are the keys to everything in our life, including our work in the classroom. We can try to teach in our own power, but we'll only accomplish so much. If we want to make a real, lasting impact, that has to come from Him. If we want to teach with the fruit of the Spirit, only He can do that in us. He is the one who knows what our students need. And He's the one that has to work in their hearts.

We know that a close relationship with God requires spending time reading His Word, praying, and thinking about His truths. But this must be more than a ritual. We must ask God questions and open our hearts to hear His response. We must know His voice so that we can hear and distinguish it in our daily lives and follow His leading.

This is a life-long process, one that's never done but that we should be continually seeking. When things get busy, however, it's easy to let prayer and Bible reading slide. When this happens, trying something new (or renewing an old habit) can help refocus our spiritual walk. With that in mind, here are fifteen ways to breathe new life into your time with God.

1. **Set aside a time to pray and read your Bible.** If we don't schedule time, it probably won't happen. Plan a daily time with God, even if it's short. Then, when you have larger blocks of free time, use them for deeper, more meaningful time with Him.

2. **Ask God questions and listen for His response.** Often we view prayer as simply a time to rattle off our wish list. But prayer should be a conversation. We should ask God what He thinks and listen to the Scripture He brings to our minds.

3. **Listen to Christian music.** The right music can help us focus on God and His work in our lives. So cue up an uplifting song and focus on it. Meditate on the words and pray as you listen or after the song is done.

4. **Watch Christian music videos.** When you're tired and fighting nodding off during prayer, jump on YouTube and type in your favorite worship songs. You'll likely find a music video or beautiful slideshows that add another dimension of meaning to the words.

5. **Journal.** Journal what you learn as you read Scripture. Writing even a few lines can add incredible meaning and impact.

6. **Write your prayers.** Writing a prayer can help you focus on what you're trying to say and eliminate distractions.

7. **Memorize Scripture.** Choose a verse or a passage and determine to read it at two to three different times a day. Find a time that is normally wasted and use that time to memorize Scripture. For example, I memorize Scripture while blow-drying my hair.

8. **Listen to Scripture.** Grab an audio version of the Bible and pop in your earbuds. Obviously, the best way to focus is to sit and listen, but you can also add Scripture to your day by listening to the Word while driving or completing other tasks.

9. **Listen to sermons.** So many wonderful sermons are available online. Try a few to find a pastor that connects with you. Then turn on a sermon while you complete household tasks. (I highly recommend Truth for Life with Alistair Begg.)

10. **Read a devotional book.** A helpful devotional book can significantly advance your spiritual life. You can read a daily devotional book like Our Daily Bread. Or, read a book on a certain topic. You may also want to check out our *Teach Uplifted Devotions for Teachers* book at **www.teach4theheart.com/devotions**.

11. **Sing.** How many times do the Psalms tell us to praise the Lord with song? Have you actually tried it in your personal devotions? You can even take it one step further by standing and adding a dance as you sing to the Lord.

12. **Go for a walk.** I love praying as I walk. You won't have to worry about falling asleep, and you have time for both praying and listening.

13. **Do a topical study.** Is there an area in which you've been struggling or a topic you want to better understand? Look up a list of verses about this topic and study them. Write down what you find.

14. **Draw.** If you love to draw (or even doodle), draw for the Lord and pray as you do.

15. Read a Christian book that makes you think. Dive into a book that will turn your mind towards spiritual things and help you meditate on Biblical truths.

Journal/Discussion: What helps you focus your prayer and Bible reading times? What new ideas do you want to try?

Lesson 40:
Fake it Till You Make It?

He gives more grace. Therefore He says: God resists the proud, But gives grace to the humble. –James 4:6

Genuine humility and authentic faith inspire respect in students, which in turn, provides an opportunity for influence. When I was in high school, we had a teacher who would get so choked up about the truths of Scripture that he would start crying. He was genuine, and we respected him for it. He had our ears, and our hearts. His impact was obvious when students who'd graduated years ago showed up to his retirement party.

We cannot put on a facade for our students—to try to be something we're not. Instead, we must be the best we can, be real about our struggles, and ask for forgiveness when we fall short. Here are seven keys to displaying humility and genuineness.

How to Be Humble and Real with Our Students

1. **Humble yourself before God.**

   You can't force humility if it's not in your heart. If you've struggled with humility, start by choosing to humble yourself before God. Seek His forgiveness, and ask Him to fill you with true humility.

2. Admit your mistakes.

When you mess up in front of your students, admit your mistake and ask their forgiveness. And I'm not talking about when you make an arithmetic error—that's easy. What's tough is admitting that you handled a discipline problem incorrectly or apologizing for losing your temper with a student.

3. Listen to advice from others.

Be humble enough to hear and consider feedback from administrators, parents, and even your students. When someone's criticizing you, ask yourself if there are elements of truth in their critique. Take what is helpful. Let go of what is untrue.

4. Think win-win.

Remember that you are on the same team as your fellow teachers, administrators, and parents—even if it might not feel like it. When you disagree about *how* to best help the students, focus on the fact that you *do* all want to help them and go from there.

5. Don't complain about others.

If you have a genuine concern, go directly to that person and express it humbly. Then, choose to give them grace and the benefit of the doubt. Don't go behind their back and complain to everyone else.

6. Don't put on a façade.

Don't tell your students to do or be something that you're not, and don't pretend to be someone different than you are. Sometimes we think that to be professional we must put on a persona when we step into the classroom. In one sense, yes, we must act professionally and command respect, but the problem comes when we try to put on a front—to be something we're not. That doesn't ring true. Instead, we need to recognize our new role—that of mentor and teacher—and bring our genuine self and personality to that new role.

7. **Be real about your struggles.**

None of us are perfect, so don't pretend to be. Share your struggles with your students (when appropriate), and discuss how you work through them. When you're real about your struggles and demonstrate a growth mindset, you not only build powerful rapport, but you also demonstrate to your students how they can learn and mature as well.

Journal/Discussion: Why are humility and genuineness so powerful in the classroom?

Lesson 41:
Teach for the Heart

When I completed my student teaching, I was struck by a
fascinating conundrum. The classroom management at this
school was, on one hand, impeccable. Due to the strictly-enforced
policy that even one word of unpermitted chatter resulted in
an immediate detention, there were few classroom issues. Yet I
couldn't help but wonder, were these perfectly quiet and orderly
classrooms a true indication of the state of the students' hearts? Or
were we simply white-washing the walls, creating an environment
where we could teach without distraction, but ignoring the real
challenges and heart issues that brewed right below the surface?

If we want to make a lasting difference, one that will impact
students for the long run, we must be concerned not only with
our students' outward behavior but also with what's in their hearts.
It's much easier to force a certain outward behavior, but that only
lasts until they walk out the school doors. The only way to have
a life-long impact is to change the way they think by teaching for
the heart.

To do this, we must first choose to care more about our students'
hearts than their outward behavior. We cannot only focus on
having a quiet class so that if the principal walks by he'll be

151

impressed. We must dedicate time and energy (and maybe even sacrifice the perfectly quiet class on occasion) to build relationships with our students. The more they know that we care about them, the more they will be open to our help and advice. Show them you care by helping them as much as possible, complementing them, and showing interest in their lives.

As we seek to reach their hearts, we must seek first to understand, then to be understood. When there's a disagreement or a discipline issue, don't launch into lecture mode. Instead, start by trying to understand where the problem is coming from. Ask probing questions and patiently wait for their response. Often the outward behavior is simply a surface indicator of a bigger problem happening underneath. Listen for that underlying problem and address the cause instead of the symptoms. Listening and understanding their point of view first will allow you to respond to the real issues. Not only will your response be more effective, but the student will feel understood. As a result, your words will be much more likely to make a lasting impact on their hearts.

Talk with your students about their thoughts, beliefs, and attitudes, not just about their outward actions. I've seen the value of this paradigm shift most powerfully when working with my own son. As a preschooler, he would pitch horrible fits, consumed by anger over the most trivial frustrations. We tried and tried to stop the fits, worked to teach him the right response to his anger, with little success. Then one day, I realized I was treating the symptom instead of the problem. When we stopped focusing on the action (the fit) and started dealing with attitude (the anger), everything changed. With a focus on "getting the anger out of your heart" and "asking Jesus to get the anger out," the fits soon lessened and then stopped. All because we focused on the attitude—the root problem—not just the outward behavior.

As you counsel your students, use Scriptural truths when possible. In Christian schools, you can quote Scripture directly. But even in public schools you can often use Scriptural truth in your discussions without saying "this comes from the Bible." Paraphrase relevant verses naturally into your conversation, allowing God's powerful Word to work. Throughout these conversations, always speak the truth in love. Our students need to hear the truth, even—especially—when it hurts. But it must be given with love. Walk them through the scenario and patiently explain your reasoning. Avoid yelling and screaming– that's only going to make your words bounce right off instead of taking root in their hearts.

When conflict arises, think win-win, and teach your students to think this way, too. Remember that both of you want the same thing (for the student to learn and mature) instead of viewing the situation as you versus them. Draw on this common ground and show them that your goal is their good.

Above all, we must seek God's help. We must be close to Him and know His heart. We must seek wisdom through His word and His people. He often speaks through others, so make it a habit to seek advice and wise counsel. We cannot do this alone.

Journal/Discussion: How can you teach for the heart, not just force outward learning and behavior?

Lesson 42:
Making Disciples

This chapter is specifically for those who teach in a Christian school. The next chapter is designed for those in public schools.

The ultimate goal of a Christian school should be summed up in one word: *discipleship*. Discipleship means to make disciples—to help students become committed followers of Christ. For some students, that journey is yet to begin, and we pray for their salvation. Others who already have a relationship with Christ need guidance, direction, discipline, and to be taught to think from a Biblical worldview.

Discipleship doesn't happen overnight. It's a long process that needs to happen day by day to be effective. It's made of a thousand little moments that come together to produce powerful change in our students' hearts and lives. As we think about discipleship in the Christian school and how we can accomplish this vital goal, we realize it's not something we can tack on to everything else we already do. Not only is there no extra time, but it simply can't be an afterthought. Instead, discipleship must be integrated into every aspect of the day. It must become so integral that we could not separate it if we wanted to.

So to help us think in this direction, let's examine nine key aspects, to see how we should approach them to produce powerful discipleship in our Christian school.

1. **Discipline**

   Central truth: Discipline issues are opportunities for discipleship.

   Instead of viewing discipline issues as problems only, we need to view them as opportunities to guide students. When we yell at students or overreact, we ruin our opportunity, as they will likely tune out everything else we have to say. Instead, we should seek first to understand what the student is thinking by asking questions and listening. Then, using what we have learned we must speak the truth in love, counseling from Scripture as applicable.

   A soft answer turns away wrath, But a harsh word stirs up anger. —Proverbs 15:1

2. **Interactions**

   Central truth: The rapport we build opens doors for discipleship.

   You know the saying: *Students won't care how much you know until they know how much you care.* It's so true. We need to build rapport and establish relationships with students to open doors for effective discipleship down the road. Love your students and show them you care. Be both kind and firm. Be their mentor but not their friend. Be humble. Be real. Admit when you're wrong. And give extra effort to the students who are the most challenging; they're the ones with whom you need rapport the most.

3. **Spiritual Walk**

   Central truth: The only way to make a real impact is to be led by the Spirit.

   If we teach in our own strength, we will help some kids, but we will have nowhere near the impact we could if we let God work through us. We must build our own relationship with God by spending time with Him in prayer and reading His Word. We must learn to listen to His Spirit, asking God for direction and waiting for an answer. This won't happen by chance; we have to schedule this time into our day.

4. **Classroom management**

   Central truth: Without order, little learning or discipleship can take place.

   Our classroom management should create an environment that fosters learning and growth. That's why we spent the whole first section of this book learning how to keep cultivate a conducive learning environment.

   One challenging aspect of classroom management is finding a Biblical balance between mercy and consistency. We need to care more about our students than our policies. But we can't use mercy as an excuse to do nothing. Remember, God established the law before He established grace, and that pattern makes sense in the classroom, too. Establish high expectations, then listen to the Spirit to know when to give mercy.

5. **Integrity**

   Central truth: Students learn more by what we DO than what we SAY.

   If we want to disciple our students, we must first be examples of true Christianity. We must be people of integrity, which means being honest, morally upright, sincere, truthful, and trustworthy. Our faith *must* be real and genuine, all about our relationship with God and our adherence to His Word, not arbitrary standards. Above all, we must be humble.

6. **Partnership with parents**

   Central truth: God has given parents the primary responsibility for their children's discipleship; we are partners with them in this process.

   Remember that God has given parents—not us—primary responsibility for their children. Therefore, we should keep the responsibility with parents whenever possible. In our conversations with them, we should seek to partner **with** them, realizing we all want the same thing—for their student to learn and grow. In all our interactions, we must remember the Golden Rule and treat parents the way we would want to be treated.

   And these words which I command you today shall be in your heart. You shall teach them diligently to your children, and shall talk of them when you sit in your house, when you walk by the way, when you lie down, and when you rise up. You shall bind them as a sign on your hand, and they shall be as frontlets between your eyes. You shall write them on the doorposts of your house and on your gates. —Deuteronomy 6:6-9

   And just as you want men to do to you, you also do to them likewise. —Luke 6:31

7. **Lessons**

   Central truth: Leaders who think Biblically can change the world (and we can teach them how to do just that).

   Strong academics are critical not just for their own sake but also because we need Christians who are equipped to be leaders in different spheres of influence. God's truths should impact everything we explain, and we must teach our students to discern truth from error by modeling how to think Biblically. Critical thinking skills combined with a strong knowledge of Scripture will help students know how to discern and reject deception.

8. **Energy**

   Central truth: If you want to be effective, take time to sharpen the saw.

   Stephen Covey gives the example of two woodsmen working to saw down a tree. One works tirelessly, determined to finish as soon as possible. But the other pauses to sharpen his saw before resuming the work. Which one do you think finishes first?

   As teachers, we tend to run ourselves ragged, thinking we are giving our best. But we need to pause and take care of ourselves so that we have the energy and strength to give more fully to our students. We must plan and schedule time to rest, exercise, eat well, spend time with God, pray, connect with others, and grow professionally.

9. **Synergy**

   Central truth: When we work together, we make a more significant impact in our students' lives.

   Synergy means that the combined effect of everyone working together is greater than the sum of each person's individual efforts. This is especially true amongst the faculty and staff of a Christian school. Teachers and administration must work together, not in competition with each other. Think win-win, and if you have a disagreement with someone, go to them first instead of talking about it with everyone else. Work to make your teacher's lounge a refreshing haven, a place to share and exchange ideas, not to complain or criticize. Encourage each other, and ask each other for advice. Veterans, be intentional about mentoring the newer teachers in your school.

Moreover if your brother sins against you, go and tell him his fault between you and him alone. If he hears you, you have gained your brother. But if he will not hear, take with you one or two more, that 'by the mouth of two or three witnesses every word may be established.'
—Matthew 18:15-16

Journal/Discussion: Name one specific change you can make to more intentionally disciple your students?

Lesson 43:
Freedom, Religion, and the 1ˢᵗ Amendment

This chapter is specifically for those who teach in a public school. The previous chapter was designed for those in Christian schools.

Disclaimer: I am not a legal professional and this is NOT intended as professional legal advice. If you need legal advice, please seek a legal professional for help.

"I sometimes struggle with how to help my public-school students without being able to talk to them about my faith. I know a relationship with God would help so many of them. I just try to be the best example I can and hope that is enough."

This is the cry of so many Christian teachers' hearts: an understanding that our students need Christ but the realization that we cannot openly share with them the truths that could change their lives. But what if religious discussions were not quite as taboo as you might think? In fact, it is legal to teach ***about*** religion in the public school as long as you do it in an academic matter without trying to convert your students. And those legal academic conversations may open doors for God to work in ways we never imagined.

The First Amendment states: "Congress shall make no law respecting an establishment of religion, or prohibiting the free exercise thereof; or abridging the freedom of speech, or of the press; or the right of the people peaceably to assemble, and to petition the Government for a redress of grievances."

In questions of what is and isn't allowed in public schools, the focus is on the phrase "establishment of religion." This phrase was never intended to keep religion out of the government but was originally instead intended to keep the government out of religion. (If you're curious about the original intent of the First Amendment or are concerned about the separation of church and state, find out more at **www.teach4theheart.com/objections**.) None the less, the court ruling in the '60s changed how this phrase is applied in the public school system. According to current interpretation, you as a public-school teacher are an agent of the government and are not allowed to **establish** a religion.

You are not allowed, for example, to have an altar call, baptize students, or pray out loud in Jesus' name. You may not try to convert a student to your religious views or teach that your beliefs are the only correct ones. These are distinct religious practices and are considered "establishing a religion."

At the same time, you are not allowed to inhibit the expression of religion either. It is a violation of the First Amendment for a teacher to stop a student from expressing religion, to keep students from carrying Bibles, talking about what they believe, or writing a report on Jesus as a historical figure.

With all this in mind, and a remembrance that our goals as teachers should be to be a bright light pushing back the darkness, let's examine how we can (and cannot) share our faith in the classroom.

1. **Live out your faith in your daily life.**

   You are absolutely permitted to live out the tenants of faith in your daily interactions. For example, to follow Jesus' command to "Let no corrupt word proceed out of your mouth, but what is good for necessary edification, that it may impart grace to the hearers" (Ephesians 4:29) is not only permitted but is a wonderful testimony. Love your students, be patient with them, and treat them with the utmost respect as those who are created in the image of God. Live your life by Biblical principles such as the Golden Rule, and people will notice the difference—they may even ask you about it.

2. **Openly answer questions posed to you about what you believe.**

   The courts clarified that the First Amendment guarantees freedom of speech and that if you as public school teacher are asked about something related to your faith, you may honestly answer the question, as long as you're not trying to convince the student they must believe that, too. Trying to convert a student would be considered establishing a religion. But honestly answering the question about what you personally believe or practice—that's legal and is no violation of the "separation of church and state."

3. **Pray privately for your students.**

   You are absolutely allowed to pray *privately* for your students, and don't underestimate this for a second. Prayer is not this last-ditch attempt we make when we have nothing left to try (i.e. "All we can do is pray.") No, it is direct intercession to the throne room of the Almighty God who controls everything. What could possibly make a bigger difference than that?

4. **Incorporate the study of the Bible and religion into your course content.**

   As a public-school teacher, you are allowed to teach *about* religion, *about* religious holidays, and even *about* the Bible. You just can't preach or do anything that would *establish* a religion. Thousands of public high schools teach a Bible course—viewing the Bible as literature or as a study on how the Bible has impacted culture, art, or music.

   Now, to teach that the Bible is the infallible Word of God would be to establish a religion and is not permitted. But to teach *about* the Bible and how different religions view it is an academic study and acceptable. And if a *student* wants to mention that in their house they believe and practice the Bible, that is their right to speak openly, and you haven't established a religion at all. All you've done is provided a safe place for students to discuss their own views in a respectful way.

   Almost every subject brings opportunity to discuss religion or the Bible in an academic way. Literature, for example, contains a plethora of Biblical allusions that cannot be readily understood without understanding the Biblical reference. Don't shy away from these opportunities, thinking for some reason they're not allowed. They are wonderful opportunities to enrich your students' education and to bring up relevant topics of faith and religion in a right and legal way. (And remember, if students as a result of these conversations ask you what **you** think, you are allowed to answer them openly—as long as you don't try to convert them.)

   This list is extremely helpful in understanding *how* you can properly teach religion in your public school classroom (taken

from A Teachers' Guide to Religion in the Public School by
The First Amendment Center)

- The school's approach to religion is *academic*, not *devotional*.

- The school strives for student *awareness* of religions, but does
not press for student *acceptance* of any religion.

- The school sponsors study *about* religion, not the *practice
of* religion.

- The school may expose students to a *diversity* of religious
views, but may not impose a religion.

- The school *educates* about all religions; it does not *promote or
denigrate* a religion.

- The school informs students about *various* beliefs; it does not
seek to conform students to any *particular* belief.

5. **Supervise religious clubs: See You at the Pole, Good News
   Clubs, etc.** Many schools have religious clubs that are student-
   led but need faculty advisors. This is a fantastic opportunity
   not only to reach out to students but to also teach them what
   they are allowed to bring up in class. There are not restrictions
   on what *students* are allowed to discuss in these clubs because
   a teacher, as a government agent, is not allowed to inhibit the
   free expression of religion. And when the students in your
   school understand this, then they can indeed be a powerful
   witness among their peers.

   You can also attend events like See You at the Pole. You cannot
   lead prayer or the event, but you are allowed to supervise the
   event and support the students in that way. And you might be
   amazed what doors open simply by your being there.

6. Don't allow fear to paralyze you.

You may fear that if you enrich your lesson with a discussion about religion, even though it's legal, there might be parents who go to your administrator and complain. But will fear stop you from moving forward? When we realize we are full-time missionaries sent to a foreign culture in the public school, our attitude and priorities will change. When we consider eternity, dealing with an ungrounded complaint is worth it.

If you're called on the carpet, be ready with the academic reason for why you included the topic in your lesson. You as a teacher have academic freedom to enrich the curriculum, and effective teachers do this all the time. If your administrator reprimands you, realize that s/he may not even be aware of what is legal and permitted. Be prepared to kindly educate him/her, but above all, remember Biblical principles in all your interactions. Pray for those who oppose you, be respectful of and submissive to authority. Know your rights, but don't demand them. And allow your humble attitude to be a bright light that God can use to break down barriers.

Journal/Discussion: What is the key distinguisher for when religion is and isn't allowed to be discussed in public schools? How can knowing what is and isn't legal help you be a brighter light to your students?

*Much of this information was provided by Christian Educators' Association Intl. CEAI also offers a variety of services to Christian teachers in the public schools, including professional liability insurance and job action protection, and is a Christian alternative to your local teachers' unions. Find out more about CEAI at **www.teach4theheart. com/ceai** or check out our Teach with Faith, not Fear training at **www.teach4theheart.com/teachwithfaith**.*

Lesson 44:
Praying Always

As we've discussed throughout this study, prayer is more than an exercise to make us feel good about ourselves, or one more thing to check off our to-do list. Prayer is the most meaningful work we can do. While it's easy to lose sight in all the busyness and all the things that are so urgent that they feel important, one thing is needed more than all the prep work, grading, phone calls, and meetings, and that is prayer.

Remember that prayer truly does change things. It not only allows us to partner with God in His work of changing lives, but it also aligns our hearts with His perfect plan. As we finish our study, I want to provide a final list of specific things you can pray for, today and throughout the year.

1. That students will be motivated, focused, and on-task

2. That God will give you opportunities to speak truth into your students' lives

3. That there will be a spirit of unity and respect amongst your students

4. That your students will feel safe and loved in your classroom

5. That your students' families and homes will be strengthened

6. That God will keep your students safe from danger

7. That God will work in your students' lives to draw them to Himself

8. That God will keep your students from sin and its deception

9. That God will bring the right friends and mentors into your students' lives to guide and encourage them

10. That God will direct your students' future plans into the paths He has for them

11. That God will help you see your students' needs and give you opportunities to help them

12. That God will give you wisdom to properly handle various situations that arise in your classroom

13. That God will show you what needs to change in your own life and give you grace to be more like Him

14. That God will empty you of yourself and fill you with His Spirit

15. That God will give you strength and energy to do His work today

16. That God will give you a love for each of your students, especially the ones that try your patience

17. That God will give you boldness to speak truth, and love to share it effectively

18. That God will help you use your time wisely and know how to care for both your students and your family

19. That God will bring the right friends and mentors into your own life to encourage and strengthen you (and that you will be an encouragement and mentor to others)

20. That God will give you the right words as you teach so that you will be effective, engaging, and relevant

21. That you will depend on His Spirit and not on your own strength

22. That others will see Jesus in you and be drawn to Him, and that you will be a bright light leading others to Him

23. That your fellow teachers will have energy and wisdom

24. That God will give strength to the school's support staff

25. That your administration will have wisdom to make the right decisions

26. That there will be a spirit of unity amongst the faculty, staff, and administration

27. That God's Spirit will work in hearts and lives

28. That the parents will be involved and that there will be a spirit of oneness and cooperation

29. That God will direct the decisions that are being made that 30. you have no control over

30. That God will bring the right teachers, administration, staff, students, and to your school

Journal/Discussion: What are you praying today for your students and school?

Our prayer cards for teachers, complete with prayer requests and Scriptural encouragement, are available for free as part of the bonus pack for this book. Get yours at ***www.teach4theheart.com/TakeHeartBonus***.

Resources

Check out these resources to discover how to make
a bigger difference.

Teach with Faith, not Fear training

This free training, designed for Christian teachers in public
schools, will teach you how you can (and cannot) bring religion
into your classroom, help you navigate sticky situations, teach you
how to start a campus ministry, and much more.

Get started now at **www.teach4theheart.com/teachwithfaith.**

Teach for Eternity Training

Designed for teachers in Christian schools, this training will help
you grow your students' faith and create Biblical discipleship in
each aspect of your classroom.

Find out more at **www.teach4theheart.com/teachforeternity.**

Conclusion

I pray this book has encouraged your heart and given you practical tools to love teaching, despite the challenges. But let's not stop here. Continue learning and growing with us at **www.teach4theheart.com**.

And before we go, please let me pray for you:

Father, thank you for always being with us and for your promise to help and equip us to do Your work. I pray for the teachers reading this book right now—that you will strengthen them, encourage them, and provide guidance exactly where they need it right now. I pray you will give them focus and energy, wisdom and purpose, today and each day in the classroom. And may they always depend on You and invest time and energy into knowing You more. In Jesus' name, Amen.

Appendix A:
Consequence Ideas

*This list contains a variety of different ideas because teachers teach in a variety of different schools. These ideas are intended to spark your imagination. Consider things like your school culture and the age of your students when choosing consequences. What is appropriate and helpful for one situation may not be for another. We also recommend using logical consequences—consequences that follow logically from the behavior.

Have students walk laps during recess.
This is a fantastic alternative to taking away recess. It limits their fun but still lets them burn energy.

Use your school-wide discipline system.
If your school uses demerits, detentions, or office referrals, don't be afraid to use them.

Have students stay after school.
Students are required to be in your room after school for a certain length of time. This can be used to make up missing work or as consequences for inappropriate behavior.

Require students to clean your room.
The student is required to clean your room during lunch, free time, or after school.

Give Class Dojo points
Class Dojo is an incredible tool that allows you to give positive and negative behavior points. (**www.classdojo.com**)

Don't give a reward.
Plan a reward for those who meet specific behavior or academic requirements. Those who do not meet the requirements miss the reward. (This is perfect for schools that don't allow direct consequences.)

Assign discipline essays.
Instead of having students write the same sentence over and over, assign discipline essays which ask them to examine their behavior and plan how they should act differently in the future.

Call parents.
For certain families, a phone call home makes all the difference.

Keep the class after for one minute.
If the class wastes a minute of class time, hold them after class for one minute. (Consider first if this will cause problems for their next teacher.)

Hold your own lunch detention.
Require students to eat lunch in your room. Depending on the situation, you may ask them to eat quietly, complete missing work, write a discipline essay, or help you in some way.

Move seats.
Moving a student's seat is a logical consequence when they are disrupting those around them.

Only let them join a fun activity if they earn it.
Make fun activities something students must earn. Students who misbehave or do not have their work completed may miss out. You could require them to complete missing work during this time. Or pair this with the "Practice Academy" idea below.

Take away phones or have a "phone jail."
If students are misusing cell phones, take them away or put them in a designated "phone jail."

Hold "Practice Academy"
Students spend part of their lunch, after school, or other free time, practicing and perfecting the correct behavior. For example, if they throw something across the room, they practice crumbling a Kleenex, raising their hand for permission, and walking the trash to the trash can.

Make the student sit alone.
Require a misbehaving student to sit alone at lunch or in the back of the room during class.

Have students write an action plan.
Give students seven minutes to answer questions like:

1. What is the reason you are filling out this action plan?

2. What happened before the behavior? (background info)

3. What goal could you make to help with this behavior in the future?

4. Is there anything I can do as your teacher to help with the goal?

Student signs it, and you sign it. Add comments as needed; then mail a copy home and keep one on file for the student.

Plan a make-up work time.
Have a designated time for students to make up missing work.
Those who are caught up have free time or do a fun activity.

Have students take a time-out.
The goal of a time-out is not to be a punishment in itself but to
give students (especially younger students) a few minutes to calm
down, regain control, and think about what needs to happen next.
You will need to model and teach what should happen during a
time-out.

Use "you break it, you fix it."
Look for a logical consequence, a way for the student to fix what
s/he's broken. Whether they've made a mess, broken something,
or hurt someone's feelings, require them to take responsibility for
fixing it.

Withhold access to class materials.
If students aren't using class materials appropriately, they lose the
privilege of using them for a while.

Appendix B:
Call-and-Response Sayings

Teacher	Class
Class?...	...Yes?
All set?...	...you bet!
Hocus pocus...	...everybody focus.
Macaroni and cheese...	...everybody freeze!
To infinity...	...and beyond!
Hear ye, hear ye...	...all eyes now on thee.
Na na na na, na na na na...	...hey, hey, hey, goodbye.

Appendix C:
Checklist Grading Form Example

Areas circled below are areas that need improvements.
Check marks or ☺ indicate areas that were well done.

Basic Structure

_____ Contains four paragraphs that follow the correct essay structure.

1ˢᵗ paragraph (Intro):

_____ Starts by getting attention

_____ Ends with strong thesis

_____ Has at least three sentences

2ⁿᵈ & 3ʳᵈ paragraphs:

_____ Arranged either subject-by-subject (one subject per paragraph) or point-by-point (similarities in one paragraph, differences in the other)

_____ Strong topic sentences

_____ Strong concluding sentences

_____ Arrangement of points is logical and interesting.

_____ Contains good unity (All sentences relate.)

_____ Has 5-8 sentences each

4th paragraph (Conclusion):

_____ Starts with a restated thesis

_____ Does not bring up new arguments.

_____ Wraps up the essay in an interesting or thought-provoking way.

_____ Has at least 3 sentences.

Writing Style:

_____ Uses good transitional words

_____ Uses vibrant words that *show* instead of *tell*

_____ Variety in sentence beginnings (don't all begin with the subject)

_____ Words flow well and are easy to read.

_____ Uses descriptive words

Editing

_____ Spelling is correct

_____ Capitalization is correct

_____ Punctuation is correct

_____ Grammar/usage is correct

_____ No fragments or run-on sentences

_____ Formal language used (no contractions)

_____ No 1st or 2nd person pronouns used

Grade: _____

TEACH *Uplifted*

Has teaching left you stressed, frustrated, or even discouraged?

In *Teach Uplifted Devotions for Teachers*, you'll discover how to...

> Renew your passion for teaching by finding joy and peace in Christ

> Teach with joy - even in difficult circumstances

> Banish anxiety and learn to trust God instead

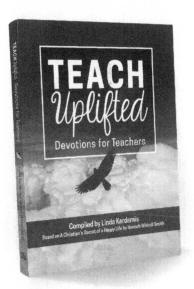

But be warned: This is not a collection of light, fluffy feel-good stories. These powerful devotions will completely transform the way you view your life, your classroom, and your relationship with God.

Teach4theheart.com/devotions

"I am LOVING the Teach Uplifted devotions. Each day I glean insight and comfort. I feel like I'll be re-reading this over and over."
    - Erin P.

83003729R00119

Made in the USA
San Bernardino, CA
20 July 2018